# A GUIDE TO THE STREET LANGUAGE OF THAILAND

# MAKING OUT IN THAI

## Phrasebook & Dictionary

Sà-wàt-dii khráp!
Hello!
Pen yang ngai bâang?
How are you?

Sà-baay dii khâ.
I'm fine.

Jintana Rattanakhemakorn

**TUTTLE** Publishing
Tokyo | Rutland, Vermont | Singapore

# Contents

# Introduction

Learning to speak a little bit of Thai can dramatically enhance your experience when visiting Thailand! Thais are naturally warm and open and they love it when foreigners make an effort to speak their language. The Thai people are very sociable and love to talk with you, but their English is often very limited. Even learning just a few simple phrases will help to put them at ease.

This book aims to have you speaking simple, practical "street" Thai right from the very first lesson—the phrases that people actually use out on the street, at work, at home and in everyday situations. With a list of these practical phrases and a few critical etiquette tips, you will find it a lot easier to speak with Thai people. In a pinch, you can quickly look up the phrases in this "mini guide" and show the Thai script versions to the person you are speaking to, in order to get your intended message across. Ready to learn Thai? Let's get started!

## BASIC INFORMATION

There are many things that make Thai straightforward for beginners:

1.  Words are never modified or conjugated for tense, person, possession, singular/plural, gender, or subject-verb agreement.

2.  Words such as "a", "an", or "the" are not used.

3.  Most Thai words are very short (and relatively easy to remember and pronounce).

Although this book focuses on casual speech, the role of formality in Thai is important. We advise you to be careful not to use very informal phrases and forms with elderly people or those in elevated positions (like monks, your bosses or clients). It is good to learn the polite forms and particles given on page 14 and only use the informal language with your friends, family, and those who are younger than yourself.

It is advisable to moderate your use of Thai slang. Although slang expressions can be useful to communicate a broad range of emotions, and thoughts, you should only use them in the appropriate situations (ordering food on the street, or talking to native speakers whom you have spent some time with and can consider to be friends). Using the wrong slang expression can make you look foolish, uneducated, and potentially disrespectful. For non-native speakers, there is a thin line between slang and profanity, and using certain words with the wrong intonation can change the meaning from "unlucky" to a "blasted idiot"!

## SOUNDS AND PRONUNCIATION

Most Thai words are single syllables, but these syllables can be pronounced with five different tones or pitches, which changes their meaning drastically. The five tones are indicated by symbols called "diacritics" placed above the vowels of the words. There are four such symbols ( ` , ^ , ´ and ˇ ). The mid-level tone has no marking above the vowel—see page 11. For example, **khaa** (mid-tone) means "to get stuck" whereas **khàa** (low tone) means "galangal" (a type of ginger). Therefore, to speak Thai correctly, you should learn to pronounce the tone and syllable combinations together as a unit. The tones and tone markings are explained on page

11 and it is a good idea to spend a few minutes with a Thai friend or acquaintance practicing them so you can "hear" the differences in pitch and pronounce them approximately. In this section, though, we will first give you some guidelines for the pronunciation of Thai vowels and consonants.

Throughout this book, romanized forms of Thai words are given to serve as a guide for pronunciation, although you need to realize that some letters are pronounced differently in Thai than in English. The written Thai script forms are also provided in case you are interested to learn them. If you have difficulty making yourself understood, you can always show a Thai person the Thai script version of a phrase.

## THAI CONSONANTS

Most Thai consonants are very similar to the English ones. There are a couple of consonants that are slightly difficult for English speakers as they are "unaspirated" meaning that the consonant sound is pronounced, but there is no accompanying puff of air. Aspirated consonants (those which have a puff of air after them) are written with an "h" after the consonant sound, i.e., "kh", "th" and "ph". When pronouncing the word "Thailand", for example, the "h" is simply a puff of air after the "t" sound, so the actual pronunciation is closer to "Tie-land" and not "Thigh-land". (In other words, the "th" and "ph" sounds are *not* pronounced as in English—they are pronounced as "t" and "p" but with a slight puff of air after the consonant.)

| Consonants | | |
|---|---|---|
| **Consonant** | **Sounds like** | **Example** |
| **g** | **g** as in go; always a hard "g" and never soft as in genre | กับ **gàp** "with" |
| **kh** | **k** as in kid, with a puff of air after the "k" sound | ขา **khǎa** "leg" |
| **ng** | **ng** as in singing | งู **ngou** "snake" |
| **j** | **j** as in jet | จาน **jaan** "dish" |
| **ch** | **ch** as in check | ฉัน **chǎn** "I" (female) |
| **s** | **s** as in send | สวย **sǔay** "beautiful" |
| **y** | **y** as in you | ยา **yaa** "drug" |
| **d** | **d** as in do | เดิน **doen** "walk" |
| **t** | **t** as in stamp, but very softly | เต้น **tên** "dance" |
| **th** | **t'** as in touch, with a puff of air added after the "t" sound (not like "th" in the) | ไทย **Thai** "Thailand" |
| **n** | **n** as in nine | น้ำ **náam** "water" |
| **b** | **b** as in boy | บ้าน **bâan** "home" |
| **p** | **p** as in spy, but very softly | ไป **pai** "go" |
| **ph** | **p'** as in pot; with a puff of air added after the "p" sound (not like "f") | พ่อ **phâw** "father" |

| Consonants | | |
|---|---|---|
| Consonant | Sounds like | Example |
| f | **f** as in <u>f</u>ine | ฟัน <u>f</u>an "teeth" |
| m | **m** as in <u>m</u>ake | แมว <u>m</u>aew "a cat" |
| r | **r** as in <u>r</u>at | เรียน <u>r</u>ian "study (v)" |
| l | **l** as in <u>l</u>ot | ลอง <u>l</u>awng "try" |
| w | **w** as in <u>w</u>ine | วัด <u>w</u>át "temple" |
| h | **h** as in <u>h</u>and | หิว <u>h</u>ǐw "hungry" |

## Word-Ending Consonants

When the following consonants appear at the end of a word, they are not pronounced clearly, but very softly (as if you are pronouncing them halfway, then stopping).

| Consonant | Sounds like | Example |
|---|---|---|
| k | **k** as in bac<u>k</u> | จาก jàa<u>k</u> "from" |
| t | **t** as in clou<u>t</u> | พูด phôu<u>t</u> "speak" |
| p | **p** as in ca<u>p</u> | ครับ khrá<u>p</u> "Yes!" |
| ng | **ng** as in ha<u>ng</u> | ลอง law<u>ng</u> "try" |
| n | **n** as in fa<u>n</u> | กิน gi<u>n</u> "eat" |
| m | **m** as in ru<u>m</u> | ส้ม sô<u>m</u> "orange" |
| y | **y** as in dr<u>y</u> | ขาย khǎa<u>y</u> "sell" |
| w | **w** as in co<u>w</u> | แล้ว láae<u>w</u> "already" |

## VOWELS

There are nine single vowels in Thai, which can appear singly or in a combination. Each Thai vowel has two "lengths": a short and a long version.

### 1. Short vowels

There are nine "short" vowels, most of which are very similar to English vowels. The only difficult one is **ue**—just remember that this is a single high vowel like **eu** in the French word **bleu** (blue) or the German ü sound with umlaut (the " ¨ " symbol above the u). It is not a combination of two vowels.

| Short Vowels | | |
|---|---|---|
| **Vowels** | **Sounds like** | **Example** |
| **a** | **a** as in c<u>a</u>r | จะ **jà** "will (v)" |
| **i** | **i** as in h<u>i</u>t | ติ **tì** "criticize" |
| **ue** | a short, high vowel like the **eu** in bl<u>eu</u> (blue) in French | รึ **rúe** "Is it?" |
| **u** | **u** as in p<u>u</u>t | ดุ **dù** "scold" |
| **e** | **e** as in g<u>e</u>t | เตะ **tè** "kick" |
| **ae** | **ae** as in c<u>a</u>t (this is a short "a" sound and not a double vowel) | และ **láe** "and" |
| **o** | **o** as in <u>o</u>nly (shorter) | โปะ **pò** "fill" |
| **aw** | **aw** as in p<u>aw</u> | เกาะ **gàw** "island" |
| **er** | **er** as in numb<u>er</u> | เถอะ **thèr** "let's" |

### 2. Long vowels

Each of the short vowels above has a "long" version, which basically means you hold the same sound for about twice as long, e.g., "awww" rather than "aw".

| Long Vowels | | |
|---|---|---|
| **Vowels** | **Sounds like** | **Example** |
| **aa** | **ar** as in f<u>ar</u>, but held twice as long | ชา **ch<u>aa</u>** "tea" |
| **ii** | **ee** as in t<u>ee</u> | ดี **d<u>ii</u>** "good" |
| **uue** | **ueue** as in q<u>ueue</u> | มือ **m<u>uue</u>** "hand" |
| **ou** | **oo** as in t<u>oo</u> | ปู **p<u>ou</u>** "crab" |
| **ay** | **ay** as in l<u>ay</u> | เท **th<u>ay</u>** "pour" |
| **aae** | **air** as in f<u>air</u> | แห **h<u>ǎae</u>** "fishnet" |
| **oh** | **o** as in c<u>o</u>ld | โต **t<u>oh</u>** "grow up" |
| **aaw** | **aaw** as in s<u>aw</u> | ขอ **kh<u>ǎaw</u>** "ask" |
| **err** | **err** as in h<u>er</u> | เบอร์ **b<u>err</u>** "number" |

### 3. Vowel Combinations

There are three other long vowel combinations, which join two vowels together, such as **ia** (ii+aa), **ua** (ou+aa), **uea** (ue+aa), and two short combination vowels: **ai** and **ao**.

| Vowel Combinations | | |
|---|---|---|
| **Vowels** | **Sounds like** | **Example** |
| **ia** | **ear** as in h<u>ear</u> | เสีย **s<u>ǐa</u>** "waste" |
| **ua** | **our** in t<u>our</u> | หัว **h<u>ǔa</u>** "head" |
| **uea** | **ua** as in d<u>ua</u>l | เรือ **r<u>uea</u>** "ship" |
| **ai** | **ay** as in <u>aye</u> | ใจ **j<u>ai</u>** "mind" |
| **ao** | **ow** as in h<u>ow</u> | เรา **r<u>ao</u>** "we" |

## Tones

Thai has five different tones or pitches, each of which gives a different meaning to a syllable. The five tones are; high, mid, low, falling, and rising. They are all written with a tone marking above the vowel except for the neutral mid-level tone, which has no tone marking.

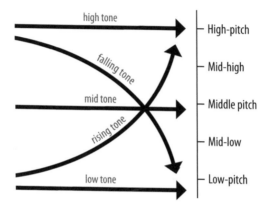

Find a Thai person willing to practice the tones with you for a few minutes. Listen to how they pronounce them then try it yourself until they say you got it right.

| Pitch Level | Symbol | Example | Meaning |
|---|---|---|---|
| high | ´ | ค้า **kháa** | trade |
| mid | no symbol | คา **khaa** | to get stuck |
| low | ` | ข่า **khàa** | galangal (type of ginger) |
| falling | ^ | ข้า **khâa** | I, slave, servant |
| rising | ˇ | ขา **khǎa** | leg |

| Pitch Level | Symbol | Example | Meaning |
|---|---|---|---|
| high | ´ | ไม้ **mái** | wood |
| mid | no symbol | ไมล์ **mai** | mile |
| low | ` | ใหม่ **mài** | new |
| falling | ^ | ไม่ **mâi** | not |
| rising | ˇ | ไหม **mǎi** | silk |

| Pitch Level | Symbol | Example | Meaning |
|---|---|---|---|
| high | ´ | น้ำ **Náa** | aunt or uncle (mother's younger sibling) |
| mid | no symbol | นา **naa** | paddy field |
| low | ` | น้อย หน่า **nói nàa** | custard apple (a fruit) |
| falling | ^ | หน้า **nâa** | face |
| rising | ˇ | หนา **nǎa** | thick (things) |

| Pitch Level | Symbol | Example | Meaning |
|---|---|---|---|
| high | ´ | ไช้ **sái** | to preen |
| mid | no symbol | ไซ **sai** | bamboo fish trap |
| low | ` | ใส่ **sài** | to wear |
| falling | ^ | ไส้ **sâi** | a filling for pastry or sandwiches etc. |
| rising | ˇ | ใส **sǎi** | to be transparent |

# Some Basics

## BASIC THAI SENTENCE STRUCTURE

Thai grammar is extremely simple. As mentioned earlier, there are no articles like "a", "an", and "the". Also, there are no plural forms, and verbs are not conjugated. Thai words never change form. The basic Thai word order in a sentence is also incredibly simple. Thai sentences follow the same "subject-verb-object" word order as in English.

No punctuation is used to indicate a question or the end of a Thai sentence. However you add short question words like **mái** "is it?" or **dâi-mái** "Would you please...?" to the end of a sentence to form a question.

When talking about quantities of things, you need to add a "classifier", similar to "four <u>sheets</u> of paper" or "three <u>bottles</u> of wine" in English. In Thai however, the number and classifier come *after* the noun = "noun + number + classifier", i.e., **grà-dàat sìi paen** = "paper + four + sheets" = four sheets of paper or **wain sǎam khùat** = "wine + three + bottles" = three bottles of wine. Adjectives precede the subject, just as in English, for example "green car" = **sǐi-khǐaw rót**.

## PERSONAL PRONOUNS

Different pronouns are used by male and female speakers. For example, to say "I" or "me", a man uses **phǒm** whereas a woman uses **chǎn**. The following are the commonly used pronouns recommended for foreign speakers.

| English Pronoun | Thai Pronoun |
| --- | --- |
| I, me | (for male speakers) **phǒm** |
| I, me | (for female speakers) **chǎn** |
| you | (polite) **khun** |
| he, she, they | **khǎo** |
| we, us | **rao** |

*Thais often prefer to use a nickname or a familial term like "mother" or "father" to address someone rather than using a personal pronoun.

## POLITE SENTENCE ENDINGS

Thais are very polite and always show great respect to some-one they have just met or do not know well by adding a respectful particle word at the end of every sentence.

- Women use **khâ** at the end of a statement or command, and this word is also used alone as a polite way to say "yes" in reply to a question. At the end of a question, they use **khá** (to pronounce this, raise your tone from the middle pitch to the middle high pitch, the same as when asking a question in English).
- Men generally use the particle word **khráp** as a polite ending to all questions and statements, to indicate respect for the person they are speaking to.

These particle words do not have actual meanings that can be translated into English, but they are like adding "Sir" or "Ma'am" at the end of a sentence. Thai people will always add them when they speak to you, and you should add them when you reply (unless you know the person really well).

# ESSENTIAL WORDS AND PHRASES TO KNOW

| | |
|---|---|
| **Hello** | [FEMALE] **Sà-wàt-dii khâ** สวัสดีค่ะ |
| | [MALE] **Sà-wàt-dii khráp** สวัสดีครับ |
| **I, me** | [FEMALE] **Chăn** ฉัน |
| | [MALE] **Phŏm** ผม |
| **Name** | **Chûue** ชื่อ |
| **My name is…** | [FEMALE] **Chăn chûue** ฉัน ชื่อ |
| | [MALE] **Phŏm chûue…** ผมชื่อ… |
| **How are you?** | **Sà-baay-dii mái?** สบายดีไหม |
| **I am fine.** | **Sà-baay-dii.** สบายดี |
| **Thank you.** | **Khàawp-khun.** ขอบคุณ |
| **Excuse me.** (I am sorry.) | **Khăaw-thôht.** ขอโทษ |
| **You're welcome.** | **Mâi-pen-rai.** ไม่เป็นไร |
| **I don't understand.** | **Mâi-khâo-jai.** ไม่เข้าใจ |
| **I don't know.** | **Mâi-róu.** ไม่รู้ |
| **Speak slowly, please.** | **Phôut cháa-cháa.** พูดช้า ๆ |

| | |
|---|---|
| **May I have…?** | **Khǎaw…** ขอ… |
| **I'm a vegetarian.** | [FEMALE] **Chǎn gin jay.** <br> ฉัน เกินเจ <br> [MALE] **Phǒm gin jay.** <br> ผม เกินเจ |
| **I'm hungry.** | [FEMALE] **Chǎn hǐw.** ฉัน หิว <br> [MALE] **Phǒm hǐw.** ผม หิว |
| **I'm thirsty.** | [FEMALE] **Chǎn hǐw náam.** <br> ฉัน หิวน้ำ <br> [MALE] **Phǒm hǐw náam.** <br> ผม หิวน้ำ |
| **I'm already full.** | [FEMALE] **Chǎn ìm láaew.** <br> ฉัน อิ่มแล้ว <br> [MALE] **Phǒm ìm láaew.** <br> ผม อิ่มแล้ว |
| **Where is the bathroom?** | **Hâawng-náam yóu thîi-nǎi?** <br> ห้องน้ำอยู่ที่ไหน |
| **How much is it?** | **Thâo-rài?** เท่าไร |
| **Can you lower the price?** | **Lót dâi-mái?** ลดได้ไหม |
| **Can you help me?** | [FEMALE] **Chûay chǎn dâi-mái?** <br> ช่วย ฉัน ได้ไหม <br> [MALE] **Chûay phǒm dâi-mái?** <br> ช่วย ผม ได้ไหม |

| | |
|---|---|
| **What time is it?** | **Gìi-mohng?** กี่โมง |
| **Can you speak English?** | **Khun phôut phaa-săa-ang-grìt dâi-mái?** คุณพูดภาษาอังกฤษ ได้ไหม |
| **What is this?** | **Nîi à-rai?** นี่อะไร |
| **How do you say this in Thai?** | **Phaa-săa-thai phôut yang-ngai?** ภาษาไทยพูดยังไง |
| **I'm feeling sick.** | [FEMALE] **Chăn mâi sà-baay.** ฉัน ไม่สบาย |
| | [MALE] **Phŏm mâi sà-baay.** ผม ไม่สบาย |
| **I'm allergic to...** | [FEMALE] **Chăn-pháae...** ฉัน แพ้... |
| | [MALE] **Phŏm-pháae...** ผม แพ้... |
| **I'm tired.** | [FEMALE] **Chăn nùeay.** ฉัน เหนื่อย |
| | [MALE] **Phŏm nùeay.** ผม เหนื่อย |
| **I'm lost.** | [FEMALE] **Chăn lŏng-thaang.** ฉัน หลงทาง |
| | [MALE] **Phŏm lŏng-thaang.** ผม หลงทาง |

# 1

# Hello, Goodbye

**Hello! Hi! Good morning! Good afternoon! Good evening!**

[FEMALE, FORMAL]
**Sà-wàt-dii khâ**
สวัสดีค่ะ

[MALE, FORMAL]
**Sà-wàt-dii khráp**
สวัสดีครับ

(informal)
**Wàt-dii** หวัดดี

When greeting another person, or saying goodbye, Thai people add the respectful endings **khá** or **khâ** (for women) or **khráp** (for men). Add these polite particles at the end of any sentence when speaking to someone you have met for the first time, is more senior or you don't know well. With younger people or good friends, you can use this conversation starter **Sà-wàt-dii** or **Wàt-dii**.

\* These polite sentence endings (**khá, khâ, khráp**) should be attached to all phrases throughout the book, except when speaking to much younger people (children) or Thais you have come to know very well over time (who are the same age).

As they say **sà-wàt-dii**, Thais will also perform the **wâi** greeting by pressing their palms together with a slight bow and their fingers extended upwards at chest level close to their body. You should always return the **wâi** as a sign of respect. (Buddhist monks do not have to do this as they are considered representatives of the Buddha.) Younger people are expected to initiate the **wâi** to their elders first. The **wâi** is not only used as a gesture of greeting or respect, but also to express gratitude and make an apology.

| | |
|---|---|
| **Haven't seen you in a while.** | **Mâi jer gan naan loei ná.** ไม่เจอกันนานเลยนะ |

**Ná** is a polite sentence ending or particle which has many uses. It can make a statement or opinion sound gentler, softer or more persuasive, or as in this case, be used as a confirmation of the previous statement to mean "Haven't seen you in a while, right?"

| | |
|---|---|
| **How are you?** | **Sà-baay-dii mái?** สบายดีไหม |

This is a common Thai greeting that literally means, "Is everything well and good?"

| | |
|---|---|
| **How is it going?** | **Pen yang ngai bâang?** เป็นยังไงบ้าง |

This phrase can also be used to ask, "How are you?" to someone you are familiar with and haven't seen for a while.

| | |
|---|---|
| **What's up?** | **Pen ngai mâng?** เป็นไงมั้ง |

Use these casual phrases to greet a person your age or friends you haven't seen for a while.

* Thai people often omit the pronoun at the beginning of a sentence when it is clear who the subject is. Thais also prefer to use names or kinship terms instead of pronouns. For example: **Mâae sà-baay-dii mái?** "How are you, mom?" or **Anne pen ngai bâang?** "What's up, Anne?" In these cases, "Mom" or "Anne" are used rather than "you".

Here are some kinship terms you can use to address people, even if they are unrelated to you.

**Older brother or sister**   Phîi พี่
(used for slightly older men or women)

**Younger brother or sister**         Náawng น้อง
(used for slightly younger men or women)

*Note that **phîi** and **náawng** can be used as personal pronouns as well as titles before someone's name. For example, a person named Malee would be called **phîi Malee** by those younger than her and **náawng Malee** by those older than her.

**Uncle**                Lung ลุง
(referring to a parent's elder brother, used for much older men)

**Aunt**                 Pâa ป้า
(referring to a parent's elder sister, used for much older women)

**Uncle or Aunt**       Aa อา
(referring to a younger brother or younger sister of your father, used for much older women or men)

**Uncle or Aunt**       Náa น้า
(referring to a younger brother or younger sister of your mother, used for much older women or men)

| | |
|---|---|
| **I'm fine.** | **Sà-baay dii.** สบายดี |
| **So-so, not bad** | **Rûeay rûeay** เรื่อย ๆ |
| **So we meet again.** | **Jerr gan ìik láaew ná.** เจอกันอีกแล้วนะ |
| **I wanted to see you.** | [FEMALE] **Chǎn yàak jer khun.** ฉัน อยากเจอคุณ [MALE] **Phǒm yàak jer khun.** ผม อยากเจอคุณ |
| **I missed you.** | [FEMALE] **Chǎn khít thǔeng khun.** ฉัน คิดถึงคุณ [MALE] **Phǒm khít thǔeng khun.** ผม คิดถึงคุณ |
| **Where have you been?** | **Pen nǎi maa?** ไปไหนมา |
| **Where are you going?** | **Jà pai nǎi?** จะไปไหน |

These traditional phrases are not meant as questions, but are often used as greetings. A straightforward answer is not always expected; you can just say **Pai-thú-rá**, which means "running an errand".

| | |
|---|---|
| **What's wrong?** | **Pen à-rai rúe plào?** เป็นอะไรรึเปล่า |
| **Nothing much.** | **Mai mii à-rai.** ไม่มีอะไร |

**I'm okay.**

[FEMALE] **Chăn mai pen rai.**
ฉัน ไม่เป็นไร

[MALE] **Phŏm mai pen rai.**
ผม ไม่เป็นไร

**I'm really busy.**

[FEMALE] **Chăn yûng mâak.**
ฉัน ยุ่งมาก

[MALE] **Phŏm yûng mâak.**
ผม ยุ่งมาก

**I'm (a bit) sick.**

[FEMALE] **Chăn mâi sà-baay nít-nòy.**
ฉัน ไม่สบายนิดหน่อย

[MALE] **Phŏm mâi sà-baay nít-nòy.**
ผม ไม่สบายนิดหน่อย

**I've got a cold.**

[FEMALE] **Chăn pen-wàt.**
ฉัน เป็นหวัด

[MALE] **Phŏm pen-wàt.**
ผม เป็นหวัด

**I'm (a bit) depressed.**

[FEMALE] **Chăn sâo nít-nòy.**
ฉัน เศร้านิดหน่อย

[MALE] **Phŏm sâo nít-nòy.**
ผม เศร้านิดหน่อย

**I'm tired.**

[FEMALE] **Chăn nùeay.**
ฉัน เหนื่อย

[MALE] **Phŏm nùeay.**
ผม เหนื่อย

| | |
|---|---|
| **I'm sleepy.** | [FEMALE] **Chăn ngûang-naawn.** ฉัน ง่วงนอน |
| | [MALE] **Phŏm ngûang-naawn.** ผม ง่วงนอน |
| **I'm sleepy.** | [FEMALE] **Chăn mâi ngûang-naawn.** ฉัน ไม่ง่วงนอน |
| | [MALE] **Phŏm mâi ngûang-naawn.** ผม ไม่ง่วงนอน |
| **That's a bummer!** | **Yâae jang loei!** แย่จังเลย |
| **That's unfortunate.** | **Chôhk-ráay jang.** โชคร้ายจัง |
| **That's a shame.** | **Nâa-sĭa-daay.** น่าเสียดาย |
| **It'll be okay.** (It'll work out.) | **Dĭaw gâaw dii kûen.** เดี๋ยวก็ดีขึ้น |
| **Cheer up!** | **Sôu sôu ná!** สู้ ๆ นะคะ |
| **What's on your mind?** | **Khít à-rai yòu?** คิดอะไรอยู่ |
| **Nothing.** | **Mâi mii à-rai.** ไม่มีอะไร |
| **I was just thinking.** | **Kít rûeay pùeay.** คิดเรื่อยเปื่อย |
| **Is Sally okay?** | **Sally oh-khay rúe plào?** แซลลี่โอเคหรือเปล่า |

**How's Sally doing?**     **Sally pen yang ngai bâang?**
แซลลี่เป็นยังไงบ้าง

You can use the same answers as those provided for the question "What's wrong?'—just replace the pronoun "I" with "Sally".

**Seen Jeff?**     **Jerr Jeff mái?**
เจอเจฟไหม

**I saw (met) Kerry.**     [FEMALE] **Chǎn jerr Kerry.**
ฉัน เจอเคอรี่

[MALE] **Phǒm jerr Kerry.**
ผม เจอเคอรี่

**Let's meet up again soon.**     **Láew jerr gan ìik ná.**
แล้วเจอกันอีกนะ

**See you later.**     **Láew jerr gan.**
แล้วเจอกัน

**Goodbye.**     **Sà-wàt-dii.** สวัสดี

**Bye.**     **Báay-baay.** บ๊ายบาย

# 2

# That's Right, Absolutely Not!

**Yes**

[FEMALE, FORMAL]  **Khâ** ค่ะ

[MALE, FORMAL]  **Khráp** ครับ

**Khâ** and **khráp** are polite particles, but they also can be used alone as a polite way to answer "yes".

To respond in the affirmative to a statement, you can use **châi**, the equivalent of "Aren't you?", "Isn't it?", or "Right?"

**No**

[FEMALE, FORMAL]  **Mâi khâ** ไม่ค่ะ

[MALE, FORMAL]  **Mâi khráp** ไม่ครับ

**Mâi** is used to say "No", but always add the polite particles **khâ** or **khráp** after to avoid coming across as being blunt or rude. **Mâi** is also added as a negative in a sentence. For example, **chǎn/phǒm mâi róu** is "I don't know" or literally, "I not know". **Mâi châi** or "no, it's not" is a standard negative reply to questions like "Is that right?" or "Is that correct?"

| | |
|---|---|
| **That's right!** | **Châi loei!** ใช่เลย |
| **You're right!** | **Khun phôut thòuk!**<br>คุณพูดถูก |
| **I think so too.** | **Khít mŭean gan loei.**<br>คิดเหมือนกันเลย |
| **I agree (!)** | [FEMALE] **Chăn hĕn-dûay(!)**<br>ฉัน เห็นด้วย |
| | [MALE] **Phŏm hĕn-dûay(!)**<br>ผม เห็นด้วย |
| **So am I.** | [FEMALE] **Chăn gâaw mŭean gan.** ฉัน ก็เหมือนกัน |
| **Me too.** | [MALE] **Phŏm gâaw mŭean gan.** ผม ก็เหมือนกัน |
| **I see.**<br>(I got it.) | [FEMALE] **Chăn khâo jai láaew.**<br>ฉัน ข้าใจแล้ว |
| | [MALE] **Phŏm khâo jai láaew.**<br>ผม ข้าใจแล้ว |
| **That's okay.**<br>(That's all right,<br>it doesn't matter) | **Mâi pen rai.** ไม่เป็นไร |

This is a common phrase that conveys the easygoing attitude of Thais. Many Thai people say this because they are fatalistic and believe that they don't have much control over things. Just accept and move on.

| | |
|---|---|
| **No problem.** | **Mâi mii pan-hăa.**<br>ไม่มีปัญหา |

Instead of just using a simple "yes" or "no", vary your speech using the following words and phrases.

| | |
|---|---|
| **Really?** | **Jing rĕrr?** จริงเหรอ |

| | |
|---|---|
| **Are you serious?** | **Phôut jing rĕrr?**<br>พูดจริงเหรอ |

This can also mean "You're joking, right?" or "You're kidding me!" **Jing** means "true', so this question is used to mean "Is it true?" In order to respond, you can say **jing** for "yes, true" or **mâi-jing** if it's not true. For more emphasis, you can repeat the word twice, like **jing jing** to express that "I'm telling the truth!" or "It's really true!"

| | |
|---|---|
| **Is that so?** | **Châi rĕrr?** ใช่เหรอ |

It means "Is that right?" or "Is what you said correct?", and is used to utter as a request for confirmation.

| | |
|---|---|
| **I guess so.** | **Nâa jà châi.** น่าจะใช่ |
| **It might be true.** | **Àat jà jing.** อาจจะจริง |
| **Maybe.** | **Àat jà.** อาจจะ |
| **Maybe not.** | **Àat jà mâi.** อาจจะไม่ |
| **That's not right.** | **Mâi nâa châi.** ไม่น่าใช่ |

| | |
|---|---|
| **I wonder...** | [FEMALE] **Chǎn sǒng-sǎi wâa...**<br>ฉัน สงสัยว่า... |
| | [MALE] **Phǒm sǒng-sǎi wâa...**<br>ผม สงสัยว่า... |
| **I don't think so.** | [FEMALE] **Chǎn khít wâa mâi châi.** ฉัน คิดว่าไม่ใช |
| | [MALE] **Phǒm khít wâa mâi châi.** ผม คิดว่าไม่ใช |
| **I'm not sure.** | [FEMALE] **Chǎn mâi nâae-jai.**<br>ฉัน ไม่แน่ใจ |
| | [MALE] **Phǒm mâi chua.**<br>ผม ไม่ชัวร |

**Chua** is borrowed from "sure" in English and has the same meaning. While **mâi nâae-jai** can be used in both informal and formal conversations, **chua** should be reserved for more casual conversations.

| | |
|---|---|
| **There's no way of knowing.** | **Mâi róu loei.** ไม่รู้เลย |
| **Because...** | **Phráw...** เพราะ... |
| **But...** | **Tàae...** แต่... |

Usually followed by an explanation or a contradiction, such as **Tàe mâi nâa châi** "But, that's not right." Here are some handy phrases for when you want to pose another question back to the speaker.

| | |
|---|---|
| **How come?** | **Pen pai dâi ngai?**<br>เป็นไปได้ไง |

| | |
|---|---|
| **What do you mean?** | **Măay khwaam wâa ngai?**<br>หมายความว่าไง |
| **Is something wrong?**<br>(because someone<br>seems different in terms<br>of mood etc.) | **Mii à-rai rúe-plào?**<br>มีอะไรรึเปล่า |
| **What's the difference?** | **Plìan pai yang-ngai?**<br>เปลี่ยนไปยังไง |
| **What?** | **À-rai rěrr?** อะไรเหรอ |
| **Why not?** | **Tham-mai lâ?** ทำไมล่ะ |
| **Are you sure?** (formal) | **Nâae-jai ná?** แน่ใจนะ |
| **Are you sure?** (informal) | **Chua ná?** ชัวร์นะ<br>(see "I'm not sure" on pg 30) |

Here are some words and phrases to emphatically express complete agreement.

| | |
|---|---|
| **Absolutely!** | **Nâae-nawn!** แน่นอน |
| **Definitely!** | **Chua!** ชัวร์ |
| **Of course!** | **Fan-thong!** ฟันธง |

**Fan-thong** is a slang term that is widely used to indicate strong agreement. It literally means "flag down" which is traditionally used in auto racing to indicate that the race is over.

**That's it!**          Nân làe! นั่นแหละ

This phrase is used to mean "that's right" or "that one" (when selecting something).

**That was good!**      Châi loey! ใช่เลย

Use the following phrases when responding to someone who says something surprising or unbelievable.

**That is too good**    Mâi yàak chûea!
**to be true!**         ไม่อยากเชื่อ

**No way!/You're joking!** Mâi mii thaang!
(a strong refusal)      ไม่มีทาง

**You're wrong!**       Mâi châi láaew!
                        ไม่ใช่แล้ว

**That's impossible!**  Pen pai mâi dâi!
                        เป็นไปไม่ได้

**Forget it!**          Châang thèr!
(I've had enough!)      ช่างเถอะ

The following are used when you are annoyed with a situation and you want it to stop.

**I don't care!**       [FEMALE] Chǎn mâi sǒn!
                        ฉัน ไม่สน
                        [MALE] Phǒm mâi chua!
                        ผม ไม่สน

**Whatever!**

[FEMALE] **Chăn mâi khaae!**
ฉัน ไม่แคร์

[MALE] **Phŏm mâi khaae!**
ผม ไม่แคร์

**Khaae** is a loanword from "care" in English. **Mâi khaae** is used to express "It doesn't matter to me", which usually carries a rather negative connotation, so be sure to use it carefully.

**I'm not interested!**

[FEMALE] **Chăn mâi sŏn jai!**
ฉัน ไม่สนใจ

[MALE] **Phŏm mâi sŏn jai!**
ผม ไม่สนใจ

# 3

# Let's Go Now!

**Got a minute?**     Wâang mái? ว่างไหม

**What time will it finish?**   Sèt gìi mohng? เสร็จกี่โมง

**What time will it end?**     Sèt tawn nǎi?
เสร็จตอนไหน

Use **sèt gìi mohng** to find out the exact time an event will likely last, or **sèt tawn nǎi** meaning "which period" of the day.

**About what time?**     Prà-maan gìi mohng?
ประมาณกี่โมง

| | |
|---|---|
| **6 a.m.** | hòk-mohng-cháo<br>6 โมงเช้า |
| **7 a.m.** | jèt-mohng-cháo<br>7 โมงเช้า |

| | |
|---|---|
| **8 a.m.** | **pàaet-mohng-cháo**<br>8 โมงเช้า |
| **9 a.m.** | **gâo-mohng-cháo**<br>9 โมงเช้า |
| **10 a.m.** | **sìp-mohng-cháo**<br>10 โมงเช้า |
| **11 a.m.** | **sìp-èt-mohng-cháo**<br>11 โมงเช้า |
| **noon** | **thîang (wan)**<br>เที่ยง (วัน) |
| **1 p.m.** | **bàay-(nùeng)-mohng**<br>บ่าย (1) โมง |

*Note that 1 p.m. can be said as **bàay-nùeng-mohng** or just **bàay mohng**.

| | |
|---|---|
| **2 p.m.** | **bàay-sǎawng-mohng**<br>บ่าย 2 โมง |
| **3 p.m.** | **bàay-sǎam-mohng**<br>บ่าย 3 โมง |
| **4 p.m.** | **sìi-mohng-yen**<br>4 โมงเย็น |
| **5 p.m.** | **hâa-mohng-yen**<br>5 โมงเย็น |
| **6 p.m.** | **hòk-mohng-yen**<br>6 โมงเย็น |
| **7 p.m.** | **jèt-mohng-yen**<br>7 โมงเย็น |
| **8 p.m.** | **pàaet-mohng-yen**<br>8 โมงเย็น |

| | |
|---|---|
| **9 p.m.** | **gâo-mohng-yen** 9 โมงเย็น |
| **10 p.m.** | **sìp-mohng-yen** 10 โมงเย็น |
| **11 p.m.** | **sìp-èt-mohng-yen** 11 โมงเย็น |
| **midnight** | **thîang-khuuen** เที่ยงคืน |
| **1 a.m.** | **tii-nùeng** ตี 1 |
| **2 a.m.** | **tii-sǎawng** ตี 2 |
| **3 a.m.** | **tii-sǎam** ตี 3 |
| **4 a.m.** | **tii-sìi** ตี 4 |
| **5 a.m.** | **tii-hâa** ตี 5 |

If you are arranging a day to meet, use the following terms:

| | |
|---|---|
| **Monday** | **Wan-jan** วันจันทร์ |
| **Tuesday** | **Wan-ang-khaan** วันอังคาร |
| **Wednesday** | **Wan-pút** วันพุธ |
| **Thursday** | **Wan-phá-rúe-hàt** วันพฤหัส |
| **Friday** | **Wan-sùk** วันศุกร |
| **Saturday** | **Wan-sǎo** วันเสาร |
| **Sunday** | **Wan-aa-thít** วันอาทิตย |
| **today** | **wan-níi** วันนี้ |
| **yesterday** | **mûea-waan-níi** เมื่อวานนี้ |

| | |
|---|---|
| tomorrow | **phrûng-níi** พรุ่งนี้ |
| next week | **aa-thít-nâa** อาทิตย์หน้า |
| next month | **duean-nâa** เดือนหน้า |
| in two weeks | **ìik-sǎawng-aa-thít** อีกสองอาทิตย์ |
| the day before yesterday | **mûea-waan-suuen** เมื่อวานซืน |
| the day after tomorrow | **má-ruuen-níi** มะรืนนี้ |

| | |
|---|---|
| **Is it too early?** | **Rew pai mái?** เร็วไปไหม |
| **Is it too late?** | **Cháa pai mái?** ช้าไปไหม |
| **When is a good time for you?** (informal) | **Khun sà-dùak tawn nǎi?** คุณสะดวกตอนไหน |
| **When is a good time for you?** (formal) | **Khun sà-dùak mûea rài?** คุณสะดวกเมื่อไร |

**Tawn nǎi** is used when speaking informally. **Mûea rài** can be used interchangeably with **tawn nǎi**, but it generally refers to a wider range of times, e.g., dates, weeks or years.

| | |
|---|---|
| **How about the 18th?** | **Wan thîi sìp-pàaet dâi mái?** วันที่ 18 ได้ไหม |

**Wan thîi** literally means "the date of". When talking about the date, you can put the following numbers after **wan thîi**, i.e., the 18th is **wan thîi sìp-pàaet**, or literally, "the date of 18".

## THAI NUMBERS 1-31

| | | |
|---|---|---|
| 1 | nùeng | หนึ่ง |
| 2 | sǎawng | สอง |
| 3 | sǎam | สาม |
| 4 | sìi | สี่ |
| 5 | hâa | ห้า |
| 6 | hòk | หก |
| 7 | jèt | เจ็ด |
| 8 | pàaet | แปด |
| 9 | gâo | เก้า |
| 10 | sìp | สิบ |
| 11 | sìp-èt | สิบเอ็ด |
| 12 | sìp-sǎawng | สิบสอง |
| 13 | sìp-sǎam | สิบสาม |
| 14 | sìp-sìi | สิบสี่ |
| 15 | sìp-hâa | สิบห้า |
| 16 | sìp-hòk | สิบหก |
| 17 | sìp-jèt | สิบเจ็ด |
| 18 | sìp-pàaet | สิบแปด |
| 19 | sìp-gâo | สิบเก้า |
| 20 | yîi-sìp | ยี่สิบ |

| 21 | yîi-sìp-èt | ยี่สิบเอ็ด |
| 22 | yîi-sìp-sǎawng | ยี่สิบสอง |
| 23 | yîi-sìp-sǎam | ยี่สิบสาม |
| 24 | yîi-sìp-sìi | ยี่สิบสี่ |
| 25 | yîi-sìp-hâa | ยี่สิบห้า |
| 26 | yîi-sìp-hòk | ยี่สิบหก |
| 27 | yîi-sìp-jèt | ยี่สิบเจ็ด |
| 28 | yîi-sìp-pàaet | ยี่สิบแปด |
| 29 | yîi-sìp-gâo | ยี่สิบเก้า |
| 30 | sǎam-sìp | สามสิบ |
| 31 | sǎam-sìp-èt | สามสิบเอ็ด |

* See page 79 for higher numbers.

| | |
|---|---|
| **When can you make it, then?** | **Láaew khun jà wâang mûea rài?**<br>แล้วคุณจะว่างเมื่อไร |
| **What time should I come over?** | [FEMALE] **Hâi chǎn maa gìi mohng?**<br>ให้ ฉัน มากี่โมง<br>[MALE] **Hâi phǒm maa gìi mohng?**<br>ให้ ผม มากี่โมง |
| **What time do we leave?** | **Rao jà àawk pai gìi mohng?**<br>เราจะออกไปกี่โมง |

| | |
|---|---|
| **What time do we arrive?** | **Rao jà thǔeng gìi mohng?** เราจะถึงกี่โมง |
| **Are you ready?** | **Khun phráawm rúe yang?** คุณพร้อมหรือยัง |
| **When will you (be able to) do it?** | **Khun jà wâang mûea rài?** คุณจะว่างเมื่อไร |
| **How long will it take?** | **Chái way-laa naan mái?** ใช้เวลานานไหม |
| **It'll only take a minute.** | **Páaep mâi naan.** แป๊บไม่นาน |
| **It'll take a while.** | **Sák phák nèueng.** สักพักหนึ่ง |
| **Next time.** (Maybe later.) | **Khraow nâa láaew gan.** คราวหน้าแล้วกัน |
| **later** | **ìik sák phák** อีกสักพัก |

There are a few ways to convey that you'll do something later. Use **ìik sák phák** when you intend to do something a few hours after the current conversation.

| | |
|---|---|
| **later** | **wan lǎng ná** วันหลังนะ |

If you intend to do something a few days or weeks later, use **wan lǎng ná** instead.

| | |
|---|---|
| **(I'll) Do it later.** | **Wái gaàwn ná.** ไว้ก่อนนะ |

This phrase is used to express that the action (i.e., work) will be completed some time in the future.

**soon** (in a few days)     **ìik mâi gìi wan** อีกไม่กี่วัน

**Ìik mâi kìi wan** is used to mean that you'll do something in a few days, e.g., **Phǒm jà pai Chiang-mài ìik mâi gìi wan** "I will be going to Chiang Mai soon/in a few days".

| | |
|---|---|
| **not yet** | **yang loei** ยังเลย |
| **not now** | **tawn níi yang** ตอนนี้ยัง |
| **the last time** | **khraow thîi láaew**<br>คราวที่แล้ว |
| **I don't know when.** | [FEMALE] **Chǎn yang mâi róu wâa mûea rài.**<br>ฉัน ยังไม่รู้ว่าเมื่อไร<br>[MALE] **Phǒm yang mâi róu wâa mûea rài.**<br>ผม ยังไม่รู้ว่าเมื่อไร |
| **I don't know now.** | [FEMALE] **Tawn níi chǎn yang mâi róu.**<br>ตอนนี้ ฉัน ยังไม่รู้<br>[MALE] **Tawn níi phǒm yang mâi róu.**<br>ตอนนี้ ผม ยังไม่รู้ |
| **I don't know yet.** | [FEMALE] **Chǎn yang mâi róu loei.** ฉัน ยังไม่รู้เลย<br>[MALE] **Phǒm yang mâi róu loei.** ผม ยังไม่รู้เลย |
| **Someday** | **Wan nǎi sák wan**<br>วันไหนสักวัน |

**Anytime is fine.**     **Gìi mohng gâaw dâi.**
กี่โมงก็ได้หนก็ได้

This means, "Whenever" or "I'm free anytime you are".

**Always**     **Dâi tà-làawt** ได้ตลอด

It literally means "I'm always available to do it".

**You decide when.**     **Hâi khun lûeak wâa wan nǎi.**
ให้คุณเลือกว่าวันไหน

**That's a bad day for me.**     [FEMALE] **Wan nán chǎn yûng mâak.**
วันนั้น ฉัน ยุ่งมาก
[MALE] **Wan nán phǒm yûng mâak.**
วันนั้น ผม ยุ่งมาก

**That day is fine.**     [FEMALE] **Wan nán chǎn wâang ná.**
วันนั้น ฉัน ว่างนะ
[MALE] **Wan nán phǒm wâang ná.**
วันนั้น ผม ว่างนะ

**Let's begin!**
(Let's start!)     **Rêrrm gan loey!**
เริ่มกันเลย

**Let's continue.**     **Maa khui gan tàw.**
มาคุยกันต่อ

**Finished?**     **Sèt rúe yang?** เสร็จหรือยัง

| | |
|---|---|
| **Finished already?** | **Sèt láew rěrr?**<br>เสร็จแล้วเหรอ |
| **I'll be finished soon.** | [FEMALE] **Chăn glâi jà sèt láaew.**<br>ฉัน ใกล้จะเสร็จแล้ว<br>[MALE] **Phǒm glâi jà sèt láaew.**<br>ผม ใกล้จะเสร็จแล้ว |
| **I've finished.** | **Sèt láaew.** เสร็จแล้ว |
| **I'll be late.** | [FEMALE] **Chăn jà pai săy.**<br>ฉัน จะไปสาย<br>[MALE] **Phǒm jà pai cháa.**<br>ผม จะไปช้า |
| **I'm here already.** | [FEMALE] **Chăn thǔeng láaew.**<br>ฉัน จะไปสาย<br>[MALE] **Phǒm thǔeng láaew.**<br>ผม จะไปช้า |
| **See you soon.** | **Dǐaw jerr gan.**<br>เดี๋ยวเจอกัน |
| **Let's meet for breakfast.** | **Maa gin khâow châo.**<br>มากิน ข้าวเช้า |
| **Brunch** | **Múe săi** มื้อสาย |
| **Lunch** | **Khâow thîang** ข้าวเที่ยง |
| **Dinner** | **Khâow yen** ข้าวเย็น |
| **High tea** | **Chaa gan** ชา กัน |
| **Let's meet for drinks.** | **Hǎa à-rai dùuem gan.**<br>หาอะไรดื่มกัน |

| | |
|---|---|
| **Shall we watch a movie?** | **Pai dou nǎng gan mái?** ไปดูหนังกันไหม |
| **Do you want to go shopping?** | **Yàak pai cháawp-pîng mái?** อยากไปช้อปปิ้งไหม |

**Cháawp-pîng** is adapted from "shopping" in English.

| | |
|---|---|
| **I'm on my way!** | [FEMALE] **Chǎn gam-lang pai!** ฉัน กำลังไป |
| | [MALE] **Phǒm gam-lang pai!** ผม กำลังไป |
| **I'll get it to you soon.** | [FEMALE] **Chǎn glâi thǔeng láaew.** ฉัน ใกล้ถึงแล้ว |
| | [MALE] **Phǒm glâi thǔeng láaew.** ผม ใกล้ถึงแล้ว |
| **I'm ready.** | **Phráawm sèt láaew.** พร้อม เสร็จแล้ว |

**Sèt láaew** literally means you've finished doing something and are now ready to go or do something else.

| | |
|---|---|
| **Let's go.** (informal) | **Pai** ป |
| **Let's go.** (formal) | **Pai gan thèr.** ปนเถอะ |

**Pai** is the most common and casual word that Thais often use to say "Let's go", while **pai gan thèr** is more formal and generally used when talking to elderly people.

# 4

# On the Road

| | |
|---|---|
| **I am lost.** | [FEMALE] **Chǎn lǒng-thaang.** ฉัน หลงทาง |
| | [MALE] **Phǒm lǒng-thaang.** ผม หลงทาง |
| **Can you help me please?** | [FEMALE] **Chûay chǎn dâi-mái?** ช่วย ฉัน ได้ไหม |
| | [MALE] **Chûay phǒm dâi-mái?** ช่วย ผม ได้ไหม |
| **Please tell me how to get there.** | **Chûay bàawk thaang nòy dâi-mái.** ช่วยบอกทางหน่อย ได้ไหม |

**Nòy dâi-mái** หน่อยได้ไหม is used to express "Please…" or "Would you please…" and is often added at the end of a sentence to soften the request.

| | |
|---|---|
| **Could you write it down?** | **Chûay khǐan dâi-mái?**<br>ช่วยเขียนหน่อยได้ไหม |

Ask your hotel concierge to write down the address of the hotel (or take their card) so you can pass it to the taxi or *tuk-tuk* (auto rickshaw) driver to find your way back, otherwise use Google Maps to get around by public transport.

| | |
|---|---|
| **I want to go to…** | [FEMALE] **Chǎn yàak pai…**<br>ฉัน อยากไป… |
| | [MALE] **Phǒm yàak pai…**<br>ผม อยากไป… |
| **Do you know the…** (name of place)? | **Khun róu-jàk…mái?**<br>คุณรู้จัก…ไหม |
| **Grand Palace** | **Phrá-baw-rom-má-hǎa-râat-chá-wang**<br>พระบรมมหาราชวัง |
| **Temple of the Emerald Buddha** | **Wát phrá-gâaew**<br>วัดพระแก้ว |
| **Temple of the Reclining Buddha** | **Wát phoh** วัดโพธิ์ |
| **Temple of the Dawn** | **Wát à-run** วัดอรุณ |
| **Chatuchak Market** | **Tà-làat jà-tù-jàk**<br>ตลาดจตุจักร |

One of the world's largest wholesale weekend markets

| | |
|---|---|
| **Damnoen Saduak Floating Market** | **Tà-làat-náam dam-nern sà-dùak**<br>ตลาดน้ำดำเนินสะดวก |

Vendors sell agricultural products and local food from their small rowing boats

**Ayutthaya**   À-yút-thá-yaa อยุธยา
The World Heritage-listed Historic City of Ayutthaya and associated Historic Towns

**Sukhothai**   Sù-khŏh-thai สุโขทัย
The first capital of Siam with many ruins from that period 1238–1438 in the Sukhothai National Historic Park

**Phanom Rung**    Praa-sàat-hĭn
**Historical Park**   phá-nom-rúng
ปราสาทหินพนมรุ้ง
A Khmer temple complex built from sandstone in the 10th century

**Kanchanaburi**   Gaan-jà-ná-bù-rii
กาญจนบุรี
The Death Railway, Erawan Falls and the Bridge over the River Kwai are located here.

**Chiang Mai**   Chiang-mài เชียงใหม่
A base for treks and for visits to temples, elephant training and hill-tribe villages

**Chiang Rai**   Chiang-raai เชียงราย
Famed for its temples, mountain scenery and cultural sights

**Mae Hong Son**   Mâe-hâwng-sǎwn
แม่ฮ่องสอน
An excellent base for trekking into isolated caves and visiting the hill tribe communities

**Khao Yai National Park**  Khǎo-yài เขาใหญ่
Great hiking trails to see the amazing wildlife, scenery, and over 293 species of birds

**Hua Hin**   Hǔa-hǐn หัวหิน
Its most famous sight is the Klai Kangwon Palace, a summer palace of the King and the Royal Family.

**Cha Am**          Chá-am ชะอำ
Discover Mrigadayavan Palace and enjoy the town's long and beautiful beach.

**Krabi**           Grà-bìi กระบี่
Crystal clear water, extensive coral reefs, numerous caves, and over 130 islands to explore

**Koh Phangan**     Gàw phá-ngan เกาะพงัน
A backpacker destination popular for its monthly Full Moon parties

**Koh Tao**         Gàw tào เกาะเต่า
One of the best diving spots in the Gulf of Thailand

**Koh Samui**       Gàw sà-mǔi เกาะสมุย
Known for its palm-fringed beaches, coconut groves and rainforest, plus luxury resorts and spas

| **Where is the... ?** | ...yòu thîi-nǎi? ...อยู่ที่ไหน |
|---|---|
| **River** | Mâe-náam แม่น้ำ |
| **Waterfall** | Náam-tòk น้ำตก |
| **Mountain** | Phou-khǎo ภูเขา |
| **Beach** | Thá-lay ทะเล |
| **Temple** | Wát วัด |
| **Museum** | Phí-phít-thá-phan พิพิธภัณฑ์ |
| **Department store** | Hâang ห้าง |
| **Coffee shop** | Ráan-gaa-faae ร้านกาแฟ |
| **Bookstore** | Ráan-nǎng-sǔue ร้านหนังสือ |
| **Movie theater** (Cinema) | Rohng-nǎng โรงหนัง |

| Hotel | **Rohng-raaem** โรงแรม |
| Hospital | **Rohng-phá-yaa-baan** โรงพยาบาล |
| Bank | **Thá-naa-khaan** ธนาคาร |
| Post office | **Prai-sà-nii** ไปรษณีย์ |
| Police station | **Sà-thăa-nii-tam-rùat** สถานีตำรวจ |
| School | **Rohng-rian** โรงเรียน |
| University | **Má-hăa-wít-thá-yaa-lai** มหาวิทยาลัย |

| How do I get to...? | **... pai yang-ngai?** ...ไปยังไง |

**Pai** literally means "to go", but it can be used to refer to taking transportation.

| **By bus** (By coach) | **Pai rót thua** ไปรถทัวร์ |
| **By train** | **Pai rót fai** ไปรถไฟ |
| **By plane** | **Pai khrêuang bin** ไปเครื่องบิน |
| **By taxi** | **Pai táek sîi** ไปแท็กซี่ |
| **By skytrain** | **Pai rót fai fáa** ไปรถไฟฟ้า |
| **By subway** | **Pai rót fai tâi din** ไปรถไฟใต้ดิน |

**Táek sîi** is a loanword from "Taxi" in English. Taking a taxi is one of the easiest ways to travel around Bangkok. Most taxis in Thailand run on meters now, but it's still a good idea to check if the taxi has a running meter before you get in, otherwise settle on a price with the driver beforehand or he may demand a higher amount when you arrive. Booking a taxi in Bangkok through a smartphone app such as GrabTaxi, Easy Taxi or Uber is useful, especially during peak hours.

Tuk tuks and motorbike taxis are also available in Bang-kok and large cities. They cost less than typical taxis, but are considerably less safe. If you decide to use either of these modes of transportation, make sure you negotiate the price in advance.

| | |
|---|---|
| **Could you take me to…, please?** | **Chûay phaa-pai thîi…dâi-mái?** ช่วยพาไปที่...ได้ไหม |
| **Which way to the hotel?** | **Rohng-raaem pai thaang nǎi?** โรงแรมไปทางไหน |
| **Go to the left.** | **Pai thaang sáay.** ไปทางซ้าย |
| **Go straight ahead.** | **Derrn trong pai.** เดินตรงไป |
| **Turn right.** | **Lîaw khwǎa.** เลี้ยวขวา |
| **Turn left.** | **Lîaw sáay.** เลี้ยวซ้าย |
| **Go this way.** | **Pai thaang níi.** ไปทางนี้ |
| **Go that way.** | **Pai thaang nán.** ไปทางนั้น |
| **Make a U-turn.** | **Glàp rót.** กลับรถ |
| **Stop here.** | **Jàawt trong-níi.** จอดตรงนี้ |
| **I'd like to go to…please.** | **Pai…** ไป... |

| | |
|---|---|
| **Can you take me to...?** | **Pai sòng thîi...?** ไปส่งที่...ได้ไหม |
| **Is your meter on?** | **Pèrrt mí-têrr mái?** เปิดมิเตอร์ไหม |
| **Please turn the meter on.** | **Pèrrt mí-têrr dâi mái.** เปิดมิเตอร์ได้ไหม |
| **How much is it to go to...?** | **Pai ... thâo-rài?** ไป...เท่าไร |

If you want to avoid the traffic, take the skytrain (BTS) and subway (MRT). Note that the BTS can be very busy during rush hours (7-9 a.m. and 4-8 p.m.). Tickets can be purchased from machines in the stations. A weekly pass can be a good option for travelers staying more than a few days.

| | |
|---|---|
| **Which line should I take?** | [FEMALE] **Chăn tâawng khûen săay năi?** ฉัน ต้องขึ้นสายไหน |
| | [MALE] **Phŏm tâawng khûen săay năi?** ผม ต้องขึ้นสายไหน |
| **Which line does it go to...?** | **Săay năi pai...?** สายไหนไป... |
| **Where do I get off?** | [FEMALE] **Chăn tâawng long thîi năi?** ฉัน ต้องลงที่ไหน |
| | [MALE] **Phŏm tâawng long thîi năi?** ผม ต้องลงที่ไหน |

| | |
|---|---|
| **Do I have to change to a different line?** | [FEMALE] **Chăn tâawng plìan săay mái?** <br> ฉัน ต้องเปลี่ยน สายไหม <br> [MALE] **Phŏm tâawng plìan săay mái?** <br> ผม ต้องเปลี่ยน สายไหม |
| **Where can I change to a different line?** | [FEMALE] **Chăn tâawng plìan săay thîi năi?** <br> ฉัน ต้องเปลี่ยนสาย ที่ไหน <br> [MALE] **Phŏm tâawng plìan săay thîi năi?** <br> ผม ต้องเปลี่ยนสาย ที่ไหน |

Get around Thailand by bus or train. Intercity buses—especially the VIP ones operated by private companies—are inexpensive and comfortable. For longer distances, trains are slower, but generally safe, convenient and very scenic—you can see lush green rice paddies and rainforests enroute from Bangkok to Chiang Mai, for example.

Thai trains have three different classes. First and second class typically have comfortable seats and air conditioning, including decent sleepers for overnight trips. Third class is fan cooled and seats are either padded or hard wood.

| | |
|---|---|
| **Where is the ticket office?** | **Hâawng khăay tŭa yòu thîi năi?** <br> ห้องขายตั๋วอยู่ที่ไหน |
| **Can I buy a...?** | **Khăaw súue...?** ขอซื้อ... |

| First class | Chán-nùeng ชั้นหนึ่ง |
| Second class | Chán-săawng ชั้นสอง |
| Third class | Chán-săam ชั้นสาม |

| Train ticket | Tŭa rót fai ตั๋วรถไฟ |
| Bus/coach ticket | Tŭa rót thua ตั๋วรถทัวร์ |
| Boat ticket | Tŭa ruea ตั๋วเรือ |

**Can I buy a ticket to Chiang Mai?**
Khăaw súue tŭa pai Chiang-mài?
ขอซื้อตั๋วไป เชียงใหม

**How much is a single ticket?**
Khâa tŭa thîaw-diaw thâo rài?
ค่าตั๋ว เที่ยวเดียว เท่าไร

**How much is a return ticket?**
Khâa tŭa pai-glàp thâo rài?
ค่าตั๋ว ไปกลับ เท่าไร

**When is there a train to Chiang Mai?**
Mii rót fai pai Chiang-mài gìi-mohng?
มีรถไฟ ไป เชียงใหม กี่ โมง

**When is there a bus to Chiang Mai?**
Mii rót thua pai Chiang-mài gìi-mohng?
มีรถทัวร์ ไป เชียงใหม กี่โมง

**What time does the bus leave?**
Rót thua àwk gìi mohng?
รถทัวร์ ออกกี่โมง

| | |
|---|---|
| **What time does the train leave?** | **Rót fai àwk gìi mohng?** รถไฟ ออกกี่โมง |
| **What time does the bus arrive?** | **Rót thua thǔeng gìi mohng?** รถทัวร์ ถึงกี่โมง |
| **What time does the train arrive?** | **Rót fai thǔeng gìi mohng?** รถไฟ ถึงกี่โมง |
| **How many hours is it to Chiang Mai?** | **Pai Chiang-mài gìi chûa mohng?** ไป เชียงใหม่ กี่ชั่วโมง |
| **Where do you get on the bus?** | **Khêun rót thua thîi nǎi?** ขึ้นรถทัวร์ ที่ไหน |
| **Where do you get on the train?** | **Khêun rót fai thîi nǎi?** ขึ้นรถไฟ ที่ไหน |
| **From which platform do I get on the train?** | **Khûen rót thîi chaan-chaa-laa nǎi?** ขึ้นรถที่ชานชาลาไหน |
| **Do you mind if I sit here?** | **Nâng trong níi dâi mái?** นั่งตรงนี้ได้ไหม |
| **Can we sit anywhere?** | **Nâng thîi-nǎi gâaw dâi châi-mái?** นั่งที่ไหนก็ได้ใช่ไหม |
| **Is there reserved seating?** | **Lûeak thîi-nâng dâi mái?** เลือกที่นั่งได้ไหม |

| | |
|---|---|
| **Does this bus/train stop at…?** | **Rót jàawt thîi…mái?** รถจอดที่…ไหม |
| **Does this bus/train pass…?** | **Rót săay níi phàan…mái?** รถสายนี้ผ่าน…ไหม |
| **I'd like to get off at…** | **Khăaw long thîi…** ขอลงที่… |
| **Could you tell me when we get to…, please?** | **Chûay bàawk dûay thâa thŭeng…?** ช่วยบอกด้วยถ้าถึง… |
| **I'd like to rent a car.** | **Khăaw châo rót-yon.** ขอเช่า รถยนต์ |
| **I'd like to rent a motorcycle.** | **Khăaw châo maw-ter-sai.** ขอเช่า มอเตอร์ไซค์ |
| **I'd like to rent a bicycle.** | **Khăaw châo jàk-grà-yaan.** ขอเช่า จักรยาน |

You can drive in Thailand with your international driver's license. In practice, car rental companies may or may not enforce this, however, you may have to pay a higher fine if you are stopped by the police without one.

| | |
|---|---|
| **What is the rate per day?** | **Khâa châo wan lá thâo-rài?** ค่าเช่าวันละเท่าไร |
| **How many days do you want it for?** | **Jà châo gìi wan?** จะเช่ากี่วัน |

| | |
|---|---|
| **How much is the deposit?** | **Khâa mát-jam thâo-rài?** ค่ามัดจำเท่าไร |
| **Do you have an international driver's license?** | **Khun mii bai-khàp-khìi săa-gon?** คุณมีใบขับขี่สากลไหม |
| **Where do I need to return the car/ motorcycle?** | **Tâawng khuen rót thîi-năi?** ต้องคืนรถที่ไหน |
| **What time do I need to return the car/ motorcycle?** | **Tâawng khuen rót gìi-mohng?** ต้องคืนรถกี่โมง |

**Rót** can be used to refer to a car, motorcycle, or any vehicle moving on wheels.

| | |
|---|---|
| **Where's the nearest gas station?** | **Pám-náam-man glâi thîi-sùt yòu thîi-năi?** ปั๊มน้ำมัน ใกล้ที่สุดอยู่ที่ไหน |
| **Where's the nearest tyre shop?** | **Ráan-yaang glâi thîi-sùt yòu thîi-năi?** ร้านยาง ใกล้ที่สดอยู่ที่ไหน |

# 5

# Eat, Drink and be Merry

Thai food is now famous all over the world and you can eat very well in Thailand for very little money. A typical Thai meal includes steamed rice, a curry dish, a stir-fried or grilled meat or seafood dish, a vegetable dish, a spicy salad, and a clear soup. All dishes are served at the same time and everyone shares. Thai cooking is a harmonious blend of many distinct tastes—sour, sweet, salty, bitter and spicy—you may even get all five in one dish! Rice is the staple at every meal—white rice in central and southern Thailand, sticky rice in the north and the northeast. Thai food incorporates influences from Laos, Malaysia and China.

| | |
|---|---|
| **I'm hungry.** | [FEMALE] **Chǎn hǐw.** ฉัน หิว |
| | [MALE] **Phǒm hǐw.** ผม หิว |
| **Have you eaten yet?** | **Khun gin khâow rúe yang?** คุณกินข้าวหรือยัง |

**Gin khâow** (literally: "eat rice") is commonly used to refer to "eating food" or "having a meal". In Thailand, having a lot of rice is equivalent to doing well in life. Rice is also depicted in local Thai culture, from folklore and rituals to paintings and sculptures.

**I have already eaten.**  [FEMALE] **Chǎn gin láew.**
ผม กินแล้ว
[MALE] **Phǒm gin láew.**
ผม กินแล้ว

**I haven't eaten yet.**  [FEMALE] **Chǎn yang mâi dâi gin loei.**
ฉัน ยังไม่ได้กิน เลย
[MALE] **Phǒm yang mâi dâi gin loei.**
ผม ยังไม่ได้กิน เลย

**Do you want to eat?**  **Khun yàak gin à-rai mái?**
คุณอยากกินอะไรไหม

**I don't want to eat.**  [FEMALE] **Chǎn yang mâi yàak gin.**
ฉัน ยังไม่อยากกิน
[MALE] **Phǒm yang mâi yàak gin.**
ผม ยังไม่อยากกิน

**I'm not quite hungry yet.**  [FEMALE] **Chǎn yang mâi hǐw.**
ฉัน ยังไม่หิว
[MALE] **Phǒm yang mâi hǐw.**
ผม ยังไม่หิว

**I'm full.**  [FEMALE] **Chǎn ìm láaew.**
ฉัน อิ่มแล้ว
[MALE] **Phǒm ìm láaew.**
ผม อิ่มแล้ว

| | |
|---|---|
| **Have you eaten lunch?** | **Khun gin khâow-thîang?** คุณกิน ข้าวเที่ยง |
| **How about dinner?** | **Pai gin khâow-yen gan mái?** ไปกิน ข้าวเย็น กันไหม |
| **What would you like (to eat)?** | **Khun yàak gin à-rai?** คุณอยากกินอะไร |
| **Do you want to eat some more?** | **Khun yàak gin à-rai ìik mái?** คุณอยากกินอะไรอีกไหม |
| **I'm thirsty.** | [FEMALE] **Chăn hĭw náam.** ฉัน หิวน้ำ |
| | [MALE] **Phŏm hĭw náam.** ผม หิวน้ำ |
| **Do you want to drink something?** | **Khun yàak dùuem à-rai mái?** คุณอยาก ดื่ม อะไรไหม |
| **Do you want to drink some more?** | **Khun yàak gin-náam à-rai ìik mái?** คุณอยากกินน้ำ อะไรอีก ไหม |

**Dùuem** "to drink" is used in formal situations, while **gin-náam** (lit., "eat water") is used in casual conversations.

| DRINKS | |
|---|---|
| **Water** | **Náam** น้ำ |
| **Iced tea** | **Chaa dam yen** ชาดำเย็น |
| **Iced tea with milk** | **Chaa nom yen** ชานมเย็น |

| | |
|---|---|
| **Hot tea** | Chaa ráawn ชาร้อน |
| **Hot tea with milk** | Chaa ráawn sài nom ชาร้อนใส่นม |
| **Black coffee** | Gaa-faae dam กาแฟดำ |
| **Iced coffee** | Gaa-faae yen กาแฟเย็น |
| **Iced coffee with no sugar** | Gaa-faae yen mâi wǎan กาแฟเย็นไม่หวาน |
| **Hot coffee** | Gaa-faae ráawn กาแฟร้อน |
| **Hot coffee with no milk** | Gaa-faae ráawn mâi sài nom กาแฟร้อนไม่ใส่นม |
| **Hot coffee with less sugar** | Gaa-faae ráawn wǎan nóy กาแฟร้อนหวานน้อย |
| **Fruit juice** | Náam phǒn-lá-mái น้ำผลไม้ |
| **Orange juice** | Náam sôm น้ำส้ม |
| **Lime juice** | Náam má-naaw น้ำมะนาว |
| **Coconut juice** | Náam má-phráaw น้ำมะพร้าว |
| **Milk** | Nom นม |
| **Soda** | Soh daa โซดา |
| **Coke** | Khóhk โค้ก |
| **Beer** | Bia เบียร์ |
| **Red wine** | Waai daeng ไวน์แดง |

| | |
|---|---|
| **White wine** | Waai khǎow ไวน์ขาว |
| **Liquor/whisky** | Lâo เหล้า |

**Dùuem** can also refer to alcoholic drinks as in the following sentences.

**I don't want to drink.** 　[FEMALE] **Chǎn mâi châawp dùuem.** ฉัน ไม่ชอบดื่ม

[MALE] **Phǒm mâi châawp dùuem.** ผม ไม่ชอบดื่ม

**I won't drink.** 　[FEMALE] **Chǎn mâi dùuem.** ฉัน ไม่ดื่ม

[MALE] **Phǒm mâi dùuem.** ผม ไม่ดื่ม

**I can't drink.** 　[FEMALE] **Chǎn dùuem mâi dâi.** ฉัน ดื่มไม่ได้

[MALE] **Phǒm dùuem mâi dâi.** ผม ดื่มไม่ได้

**Thank you, but I still have some left.** 　[FEMALE] **Khàawp khun tàae chǎn yang dùuem mòt.** ขอบคุณ แต่ ฉัน ยัง ดื่ม ไม่หมด

[MALE] **Khàawp khun tàae phǒm yang gin mâi mòt.** ขอบคุณ แต่ ผม ยัง กิน ไม่หมด

| | |
|---|---|
| **Drink a little bit more.** | **Dùuem ìik nòy ná.**<br>ดื่มอีกหน่อยนะ |
| **I'm already drunk.** | [FEMALE] **Chăn mao láaew.**<br>ฉัน เมาแล้ว<br>[MALE] **Phŏm mao láaew.**<br>ผม เมาแล้ว |
| **I am not drunk yet.** | [FEMALE] **Chăn yang mâi mao.**<br>ฉัน ยังไม่เมา<br>[MALE] **Phŏm yang mâi mao.**<br>ผม ยังไม่เมา |

There are a few ways to propose a toast in Thai. There's **Chon gâaew** which literally means "touch glasses" or more simply just **Chon!** so that everyone at a table will raise their glasses.

| | |
|---|---|
| **Cheers!** | **Chon gâaew** ชนแก้ว |
| **Bottoms up** | **Mòt gâaew** หมดแก้ว |

The legal drinking age in Thailand is 20 years old. Bars occasionally check IDs for tourists. Drugs do happen in Thailand, so be careful about taking drinks from strangers or leaving a drink unattended. With one of the highest drinking-and-driving problems in the world, Thailand is putting increasing pressure on alcohol sales and account-ability throughout the country.

Alcohol sales are prohibited during provincial and national elections, Buddhist holidays, and certain public holidays such as the King's birthday.

Bar closing times are set at midnight in many places through-out Thailand. Minimarts (such as 7-Eleven) and grocery stores are only legally allowed to sell alcohol from 11 a.m. to 2 p.m. and from 5 p.m. until midnight.

## USEFUL PHRASES IN A RESTAURANT

**May I have a menu, please?**  Khǎaw may-nou nòy?
ขอเมนูหน่อย

**What's good here?**  Thîi nîi à-rai à-ròy?
ที่นี่อะไรอร่อย

**I'd like ...** (Thai dishes)  Khǎaw... ขอ...

## COMMON THAI DISHES

**Pad Thai**
(stir-fried rice noodle)  Phàt-thai ผัดไทย

**Green curry**
(usually sweet and mildly spicy)  Gaeng khîaw wǎan
แกงเขียวหวาน

**Spicy shrimp soup**  Tôm yam gûng ต้มยำกุ้ง

**Red curry paste with chicken**  Phá-naeng gài
พะแนงไก่

**Coconut soup with galangal and chicken**  Tôm khàa gài ต้มข่าไก่

**Chicken with cashews**  Gài phàt mét má-mûang
ไก่ผัดเม็ดมะม่วง

**Sweet and sour chicken**  Phàt prîaw wǎan gài
ผัดเปรี้ยวหวานไก่

**Omelet with minced pork**  Khai jiaw mǒu sàp
ไข่เจียวหมูสับ

**Grilled chicken**  Gài yâang ไก่ย่าง

**Deep-fried chicken**  Gài thâawt ไก่ทอด

| | |
|---|---|
| **Deep-fried pork and garlic** | **Mǒu thâawt grà-thiam** หมูทอดกระเทียม |
| **Minced pork with sweet basil** | **Phàt grà-phrao mǒu** ผัดกะเพราหมู |
| **Stir fried mixed vegetables** | **Phàt phàk ruam** ผัดผักรวม |
| **Green papaya spicy salad** | **Sôm tam**  ส้มตำ |
| **Sticky rice** | **Khâow nǐaw** ข้าวเหนียว |
| **White rice** | **Khâow** ข้าว |
| **Fried rice** | **Khâow phàt** ข้าวผัด |
| **Beef noodle soup** | **Gǔay-tǐaw nûea** ก๋วยเตี๋ยวเนื้อ |
| **Chicken noodle soup** | **Gǔay-tǐaw gài** ก๋วยเตี๋ยวไก่ |

| | |
|---|---|
| **Don't add any...** | **Mâi sài...** ไม่ใส่... |

| | |
|---|---|
| **Pork** | **Mǒu** หมู |
| **Chicken** | **Gài** ไก่ |
| **Fish** | **Plaa** ปลา |
| **Shrimp** | **Gûng** กุ้ง |
| **Mussels** | **Hǒy** หอย |
| **Seafood** | **Aa-hǎan thá-lay** อาหารทะเล |
| **Peanuts** | **Thùa** ถั่ว |

| | |
|---|---|
| **Fish sauce** | Náam plaa น้ำปลา |
| **Chili peppers** | Phrík พริก |
| **Sugar** | Náam taan น้ำตาส |

| | |
|---|---|
| **Not too spicy, please.** | Mâi phêt mâak ná. ไม่เผ็ดมากนะ |
| **What's your favorite food?** | Khun châawp gin à-rai? คุณชอบกินอะไร |
| **Can you eat spicy food?** | Khun gin phèt dâi mái? คุณกินเผ็ดได้ไหม |
| **Yes, I can.** | [FEMALE] Chăn gin dâi. ฉัน กินได้ |
| | [MALE] Phŏm gin dâi. ผม กินได้ |
| **No, I can't.** | [FEMALE] Chăn gin mâi dâi. ฉัน กินไม่ได้ |
| | [MALE] Phŏm gin mâi dâi. ผม กินไม่ได้ |
| **What's it called?** | An-níi rîak à-rai? อันนี้เรียกอะไร |
| **I've never tried...** | [FEMALE] Chăn yang mâi koey gin... ฉัน ยังไม่เคยกิน... |
| | [MALE] Phŏm yang mâi koey gin... ผม ยังไม่เคยกิน... |

| | |
|---|---|
| **Does this have...?** | **Jaan níi mii...mái?**<br>จานนี้มี...ไหม |
| **I'm allergic to...** | [FEMALE] **Chǎn pháae...**<br>ฉัน แพ้... |
| | [MALE] **Phǒm pháae...**<br>ผม แพ้... |
| **I'm a vegan.** | [FEMALE] **Chǎn gin jay.**<br>ฉัน กินเจ |
| **I'm a vegetarian.** | [MALE] **Phǒm mang-sà-wí-rát.**<br>ผม มังสวิรัติ |

In Thailand there are two terms used to describe vegetarian food. The easiest way is to say **Jay**, which indicates that you are a strict vegan—your food cannot have meat, animal products, garlic, onions, and strong spices. Use **mang-sà-wí-rát** to indicate that you're a vegetarian who can eat eggs and dairy products and perhaps a little fish sauce. To ask for a dish with only vegetables and no meat, say **Sài phàk yàang diaw, mai sài néua sàt.**

| | |
|---|---|
| **Is this Halal?** | **Nîi aa-hǎan haa-laan chai mái?**<br>นี่อาหารฮาลาลใช่ไหม |

## THAI DESSERTS

Definitely try Thai desserts, which are usually sweet and made from various combinations of sticky rice, coconut milk, sugar, rice flour along with some tropical fruits, sweet corn or kidney beans.

| | |
|---|---|
| **Mango sticky rice** | **Khâow nǐaw má-mûang** ข้าวเหนียวมะม่วง |
| **Sticky rice with custard** | **Khâow nǐaw sang-khà-yǎa** ข้าวเหนียวสังขยา |
| **Banana pancake** | **Roh-tii glûay** โรตีกล้วย |

A doughy pastry fried in butter with a banana and egg mixture on the inside before being covered with sugar and sweetened condensed milk.

| | |
|---|---|
| **Banana fritters** | **Glûay khàek** กล้วยแขก |
| **Sticky rice in bamboo** | **Khâow lǎam** ข้าวหลาม |

Sticky rice is sweetened with black beans and thick coconut syrup and roasted on bamboo poles over low fire.

| | |
|---|---|
| **Sweet mini crêpe** | **Khà-nǒm bûeang** ขนมเบื้อง |

A set of tiny rice flour crêpes, filled with coconut cream and topped by sweet or savory Thai flavorings.

| | |
|---|---|
| **Coconut ice cream** | **Ai-tim gà-thí** ไอติมกะทิ |
| **Shaved ice dessert** | **Náam khǎeng sǎi** น้ำแข็งใส |

A combination of various jellies and candied fruits which are scooped into a bowl and topped with chunks of ice, sweet syrup and coconut milk.

| | |
|---|---|
| **Is the meal ready?** | **Aa-hǎan maa rúe yang?** อาหารมาหรือยัง |
| **We still haven't got...** | **Yang mâi dâi...** ยังไม่ได้... |
| **(That) looks delicious.** | **Dou nâa gin.** ดูน่ากิน |

| | |
|---|---|
| **It smells good.** | **Glìn hǎawm jang.** กลิ่นหอมจัง |
| **Enough?** | **Phaaw mái?** พอไหม |
| **That's enough.** | **Phaaw láew.** พอแล้ว |
| **Not enough** | **Mâi phaaw** ไม่พอ |
| **Give me a bit more.** | **Khǎaw phêrm ìik nòi.** ขอเพิ่มอีกหน่อย |
| **Another, please.** (polite) | **Khǎaw ìik** ขออีก |
| **Another, please.** (casual) | **Aow ìik** เอาอีก |
| **Is it good?** | **À-ròi mái?** อร่อยไหม |
| **It's good.** | **À-ròi.** อร่อย |
| **It tastes good.** | **Sâep.** แซ่บ |

À-ròy is commonly used to express "delicious or tasty" in both formal and informal setting. If you want to say "It's really good/tasty", you can add other words, such as à-ròy mâak mâak, à-ròy sùt sùt, or sâep, (taken from the North-Eastern Thai or Isaan dialect and used as a slang).

| | |
|---|---|
| **It's okay.** | **O.K.** โอเค้ |
| **So-so.** | **Phaw dâi.** พอได้ |

"O.K." is borrowed from English, and both words are used to indicate "adequate" in terms of food satisfaction.

**It's not good.**     **Mâi à-ròy.** ไม่อร่อย

Try not to use this phrase even if you don't like the food. It's better to say "It's okay" or "so so" to avoid causing offence.

**May I have the bill, please?**     **Khít ngern?** คิดเงิน

**Check, please.**     **Chék bin** เช็คบิล

**Chék bin** is adapted from "Check, please/Bill, please" in English, while **khít ngern** literally means to "charge (money) for".

* In a restaurant in Thailand, most waiters/waitresses expect get a tip (about 20-50 Baht), unless you go to a basic local restaurant (or a street stall). Some restaurants already include the service charge to the bill, so you don't need to leave an additional tip, unless you really want to.

**Let's split the bill.**     **Hăan gan jàay.**
หารกันจ่าย

**Let's go Dutch.**     **Hăan yáek jàay.**
หารแยกจ่าย

**Let me pay.**     [FEMALE] **Chăn líang eng.**
ฉัน เลี้ยงเอง

**It's my treat.**     [MALE] **Phŏm líang eng.**
ผม เลี้ยงเอง

## WHERE TO EAT

Apart from restaurants, here are a few different choices where you can grab a bite or find regional and seasonal food.

**Street food stalls** are convenient and cheap. Some street vendors operate in groups with their own set of tables, especially in local markets, so you have a variety of choices. They sell pre-cooked and made-to-order food. If you are concerned about your digestive system, here are a few tips: Request made-to-order dishes that are stir-fried and cooked in front of you, or grilled skewers of meat, or soups that are boiling in a pot. These may include a bowl or plate of noodles. Below are some examples of popular street food dishes you'll likely find everywhere in Thailand.

| | |
|---|---|
| **Pad Thai** | **Phàt-Thai** ผัดไทย |
| **Fried rice with pork** | **Khâow-phàt mǒu** ข้าวผัด หมู |
| **Fried rice with chicken** | **Khâow-phàt gài** ข้าวผัด ไก |
| **Fried rice with shrimp** | **Khâow-phàt gûng** ข้าวผัด กุ้ง |
| **Fried rice with crab** | **Khâow-phàt pou** ข้าวผัด ปู |
| **Grilled chicken** | **Gài-yâang** ไก่ย่าง |
| **Papaya salad** | **Sôm-tam** ส้มตำ |
| **Pork skewers with sticky rice** | **Mǒu-pîng gàp khâow-nǐaw** หมูปิ้งกับข้าวเหนียว |
| **Egg noodle soup** | **Bà-mìi-náam** บะหมี่น้ำ |

| | |
|---|---|
| **Steamed chicken on rice** | **Khâow-man-gài** ข้าวมันไก่ |
| **Stir-fried pork with holy basil** | **Phàt gà-phrao mǒu** ผัดกะเพราหมู |
| **Thai spring rolls** | **Paaw-pía thâwt** ปอเปี๊ยะทอด |
| **Flat rice noodle stir-fried with eggs** | **Phàt-sii-éw** ผัดซีอิ๊ว ผัดซีอิ๊ว |
| **Thai boat noodles** (contains cow's or pig's blood mixed in the soup) | **Gǔay-tǐaw-ruea** ก๋วยเตี๋ยวเรือ |

**Food courts** in Thailand are found in many shopping centers like MBK (**Mahboonkrong**) Center, usually in the basement or on one of the upper floors. These serve a multitude of freshly-cooked dishes. Every food court in Thailand must pass a sanitation inspection so you can eat without worry.

**Mobile street stalls** are motorcycles with a side car selling grilled snacks. Popular dishes include sun-dried squid, meats on skewers, and grilled sausages, or deep-fried snacks such as fried insects or fried sausages. Peeled and sliced fruits are also sold from street carts, laid out on a bed of crushed ice.

## 6

# Hitting the Shops

Thailand is a great place for shopping. You will find everything here from mega shopping malls to local markets, night markets, department stores, and independent boutiques. Shopping malls—including EmQuatier, Siam Discovery, Siam Paragon and the Platinum Fashion Mall—usually have great food courts, restaurants and cafés, bookstores, accessories, trendy fashion boutiques and specialty stores. These shopping centers are clustered together within a fairly small area, which you can either walk to or take the BTS (Skytrain). In contrast, there are also plenty of open-air shopping malls and markets, such as Chatuchak Market, Khao San Road, Asiatique the Riverfront, K Village, Pratunam Market, and Patpong Night Market. The items here are cheap but may not be of great quality.

Bangkok can also be an affordable place to custom-make clothes, especially suits, trousers and shirts. A few good places to go are: Empire Tailors, Universal Tailors, Tailor on Ten and Rajawongse Tailors. Prices for shirts start at 1,500 baht, while full suits range from 10,000 baht upwards. The tailor will need 3-5 days to ensure a fit is perfect for you.

It is common to bargain in markets and small tourist souvenir stores, but not in convenience stores or upscale shopping malls. Check out the prices in a few different stores before buying, and ask for a discount if you are buying a lot.

## THAI NUMBERS

| | | |
|---|---|---|
| 0 | sǒun | ศูนย์ |
| 1 | nùeng | หนึ่ง |
| 2 | sǎawng | สอง |
| 3 | sǎam | สาม |
| 4 | sìi | สี่ |
| 5 | hâa | ห้า |
| 6 | hòk | หก |
| 7 | jèt | เจ็ด |
| 8 | pàaet | แปด |
| 9 | gâo | เก้า |
| 10 | sìp | สิบ |
| 11 | sìp-èt | สิบเอ็ด |
| 12 | sìp-sǎawng | สิบสอง |
| 20 | yîi-sìp | ยี่สิบ |
| 21 | yîi-sìp-èt | ยี่สิบเอ็ด |
| 30 | sǎam-sìp | สามสิบ |
| 31 | sǎam-sìp-èt | สามสิบเอ็ด |

| 100 | nùeng-róy | หนึ่งร้อย |
|---|---|---|
| 101 | nùeng-róy-èt | หนึ่งร้อยเอ็ด |
| 102 | nùeng-róy-săawng | หนึ่งร้อยสอง |
| 110 | nùeng-róy-sìp | หนึ่งร้อยสิบ |
| 200 | săawng-róy | สองร้อย |
| 1,000 | nùeng-phan | หนึ่งพัน |
| 1,010 | nùeng-phan-sìp | หนึ่งพันสิบ |
| 1,100 | nùeng-phan nùeng-róy | หนึ่งพัน หนึ่งร้อย |
| 1,101 | nùeng-phan nùeng-róy-èt | หนึ่งพัน หนึ่งร้อยเอ็ด |
| 2,000 | săawng-phan | สองพัน |
| 10,000 | nùeng-mùuen | หนึ่งหมื่น |
| 10,010 | nùeng-mùuen-sìp | หนึ่งหมื่นสิบ |
| 100,000 | nùeng-săaen | หนึ่งแสน |
| 100,010 | nùeng-săaen-sìp | หนึ่งแสนสิบ |
| 1,000,000 | nùeng-láan | หนึ่งล้าน |
| 1,000,010 | nùeng-láan-sìp | หนึ่งล้านสิบ |

**Let's go shopping!**     **Pai cháawp-pîng gan!**
ไปช้อปปิ้งกัน

**Let's go buy things.**     **Pai súue khăawng gan.**
ไปซื้อของกัน

The word **cháawp-pîng** is borrowed from "shopping" in
English and is specifically used when shopping at a mall,

market or department store. If you're buying goods or food at a local shop, market, supermarket, grocery, kiosk, or convenient store, simply say **pai súue khǎawng**, which literally means, "go buy things".

| | |
|---|---|
| **What are you looking for?** | **Khun yàak súue à-rai?** คุณอยากซื้ออะไร |
| **I'm looking for a dress.** | [FEMALE] **Chǎn yàak dou sûea-phâa?** ฉัน อยากดูเสื้อผ้า |
| **I'm looking for a shirt.** | [MALE] **Phǒm yàak dou sûea?** ผม อยากดูเสื้อ |
| **Where should we shop?** (shop or buy) | **Rao pai súue thîi-nǎi dii?** เราไป ดู ที่ไหนดี |
| **Where should we shop?** (window shopping) | **Rao pai dou thîi-nǎi dii?** เราไป ซื้อ ที่ไหนดี |

**Súue** is used to mean "to shop or to buy", while **dou** (lit., "look for") can be used to refer to window shopping.

| | |
|---|---|
| **Do you want to go to a shopping centre or a market?** | **Khun yàak pai hâang rǔue tà-làat?** คุณอยากไปห้างหรือตลาด |

## USEFUL PHRASES FOR SHOPPING

| | |
|---|---|
| **How much is it?** | **Thâo rài?** เท่าไร |
| **How much is this shirt?** | **Sûea thâo-rài?** เสื้อเท่าไร |

| It's too expensive! | **Phaeng pai nòy!** |
|---|---|
| | แพงไปหน่อย |

This literally means "It's a little too expensive". Instead of using this phrase, which might offend the vendor, it is better to ask for a discount.

| **Can you lower the price please?** | **Lót dâi-mái?** ลดได้ไหม |
|---|---|

## BARGAINING TACTICS

Here are some tips for haggling in Thailand.

In tourist areas, for example Khao San Road, aim for a discount of 30-40% off the opening price, whereas in other places a 10-20% discount may be more realistic.

If you are not getting the price you want, you can politely say **khàwp khun** (thank you) and walk out of the store. Sometimes the vendor will call you back and agree to your price if your offer is reasonable.

| **Can you give (me) a bigger discount?** | **Lót ìik nòy dâi-mái?** |
|---|---|
| | ลดอีกหน่อยได้ไหม |

| **Is there a discount if I buy more?** | **Súue yér lót ìik dâi-mái?** |
|---|---|
| | ซื้อเยอะลดอีกได้ไหม |

| **What is your best price?** | **Lót dâi tem thîi thâo-rài?** |
|---|---|
| | ลดได้เต็มที่เท่าไร |

| | |
|---|---|
| **I don't have any money left.** | [FEMALE] **Chăn mii ngern mâi phaaw.** ฉัน มีเงินไม่พอ<br>[MALE] **Phŏm mii ngern mâi phaaw.** ผม มีเงินไม่พอ |
| **I didn't get enough change.** | [FEMALE] **Chăn mii ngern thaawn mâi phaaw.** ฉัน มีเงินทอนไม่พอ<br>[MALE] **Phŏm mii ngern thaawn mâi phaaw.** ผม มีเงินทอนไม่พอ |
| **Can you break this note into smaller bills?** | **Khăaw láaek báaeng yôy dâi-mái?** ช่วยแลกแบงค์ย่อย ได้ไหม |
| **Do you accept credit cards?** | **Ráp bàt khray-dìt măi?** คุณรับบัตรเครดิตไหม |
| **Can I try this on?** | **Lawng dâi-mái?** ลองได้ไหม |
| **Where's the changing room?** | **Hâawng laawng yòu thîi năi?** ห้องลองอยู่ที่ไหน |
| **Do you have a mirror?** | **Mii grà jòk mái?** มีกระจกไหม |
| **It's too big.** | **Yài pai nòy.** ใหญ่ไปหน่อย |

**Nòy** literally means "a bit", "somewhat" or " to some extent" and is often added at the end of sentences to soften the meaning and make it more polite. So, in this phrase it is used to express "It's a little too big".

| | |
|---|---|
| **Do you have a smaller size?** | **Mii lék gwàa níi mái?** มีเล็กกว่านี้ไหม |
| **It's too small.** | **Lék pai nòy.** เล็กไปหน่อย |
| **Do you have a larger size?** | **Mii yài gwàa níi mái?** มีใหญ่กว่านี้ไหม |
| **Do you have any other colors?** | **Mii sĭi ùen mái?** มีสีอื่นไหม |

| | |
|---|---|
| **black** | **sĭi dam** สีดำ |
| **red** | **sĭi daaeng** สีแดง |
| **white** | **sĭi khăow** สีขาว |
| **navy blue** | **sĭi náam-ngern** สีน้ำเงิน |
| **blue** | **sĭi fáa** สีฟ้า |
| **yellow** | **sĭi lŭeang** สีเหลือง |
| **orange** | **sĭi sôm** สีส้ม |
| **green** | **sĭi khĭaw** สีเขียว |
| **pink** | **sĭi chom-phou** สีชมพู |
| **purple** | **sĭi mûang** สีม่วง |
| **brown** | **sĭi náam-taan** สีน้ำตาล |
| **gray** | **sĭi thao** สีเทา |

| | |
|---|---|
| **Do you have shoes as well?** | **Mii raawng-tháo dûay mái?** มีรองเท้าด้วยไหม |
| **I like this one.** | [FEMALE] **Chăn châawp an níi.** ฉัน ชอบอันนี้ |
| | [MALE] **Phŏm châawp an níi.** ผม ชอบอันนี้ |
| **I will take this one.** | [FEMALE] **Chăn aow an níi.** ฉัน เอาอันน |
| | [MALE] **Phŏm aow an níi.** ผม เอาอันน |
| **I will buy this.** | [FEMALE] **Chăn súue an níi.** ฉัน ซื้ออันน |
| | [MALE] **Phŏm súue an níi.** ผม ซื้ออันน |
| **It's so cute.** | **Nâa rák mâak.** น่ารักมาก |
| **It's so pretty.** (for women) | **Sŭay mâak.** สวยมาก |
| **It's cool.** (It's stylish.) (for men and women) | **Thê mâak.** เท่มาก |

**Sŭay** means beautiful, pretty and gorgeous and is used for women, their clothes, and accessories etc. **Thê**, meaning cool or stylish can be used for both men and women.

| **This is not nice.** | **Mâi sŭay.** ไม่สวย |
|---|---|

In some cases, **sŭay** can be used when talking about general objects and views.

| It doesn't fit me. | [FEMALE] **Chăn sài mâi phaaw dii.**<br>ฉัน ใส่ไม่พอดี |
| | [MALE] **Phŏm sài mâi phaaw dii.**<br>ผม ใส่ไม่พอดี |
| It doesn't look good on me. | [FEMALE] **Chăn sài mâi sŭay.**<br>ฉันใส่ไม่สวย |
| It's not me. | [MALE] **Mâi khâo gàp phŏm.**<br>ไม่เข้ากับผม |
| It's not my style. | [FEMALE] **Mâi châi sà-taai khăawng chăn.**<br>ไม่ใช่สไตล์ของฉัน |
| | [MALE] **Mâi châi sà-taai khăawng phŏm.**<br>ไม่ใช่สไตล์ของผม |

**Sà-taai** is adopted from "style" in English.

When you're still not sure if you want to buy the item that the vendor shows you, use the following phrases with a smile before leaving.

| I'm going to look around. | **Khăaw derrn dou gàwn.**<br>ขอเดินดูก่อน |
| Let me think about it. | **Khăaw khít dou gàwn.**<br>ขอคิดดูก่อน |
| I'll come back later. | **Dĭaw jà glàp maa mài.**<br>เดี๋ยวจะกลับมาใหม่ |

# 7

# Tech Talk

## GETTING INTERNET ACCESS

The Internet is widely available in major cities in Thailand, but still not that common in remote rural areas. You can get free Internet access or Wi-Fi in most hotels, guesthouses, cafés, modern restaurants, bars or Internet cafés.

To stay connected in Thailand, buy a prepaid tourist SIM card for between 199-799 baht, which offers unlimited Internet access and special international call rates. You can easily purchase a SIM card at telecom shops or any 7-Eleven or Family Mart convenience stores, as well as at airport kiosks. There are three main network companies—AIS, DTAC and True. Check prices and compare plans and packages before buying. You'll also be able to access your network company's Wi-Fi hotspots for free on your devices for up to 30 days, depending on the package you purchase. Here are some Thai phrases and terms to help you get Internet access.

| | |
|---|---|
| **Do you have a Wi-Fi connection?** | **Khun mii waai-faai mái?** คุณมีวายฟายไหม |

| | |
|---|---|
| **May I get Internet access please?** | **Khǎaw chái In-ter-nèt dâi-mái?**<br>ขอ ใช้อินเตอร์เน็ต ได้ไหม |
| **May I get the Wi-Fi password please?** | **Khǎaw rá-hàt waai-faai dâi-mái?**<br>ขอ รหัสวายฟาย ได้ไหม |
| **May I use the computer please?** | **Khǎaw chái cawm-phíew-têr dâi-mái?**<br>ขอ ใช้คอมพิวเตอร์ ได้ไหม |

*Cawm-phíew-têr is a loanword and can refer to both laptops and computer notebooks.

| | |
|---|---|
| **I can't get access to the Internet.** | [FEMALE] **Chǎn khâo In-ter-nèt mâi-dâi.**<br>ฉัน เข้าอินเตอร์เน็ต ไม่ได้<br><br>[MALE] **Phǒm khâo In-ter-nèt mâi-dâi.**<br>ผม เข้าอินเตอร์เน็ต ไม่ได้ |
| **I can't connect to Wi-Fi.** | [FEMALE] **Chǎn khâo In-ter-nèt mâi-dâi.**<br>ฉัน เข้าอินเตอร์เน็ต ไม่ได้<br><br>[MALE] **Phǒm khâo In-ter-nèt mâi-dâi.**<br>ผม เข้าอินเตอร์เน็ต ไม่ได้ |

| | |
|---|---|
| **I can't send an email.** | [FEMALE] **Chăn sòng ii-meo mâi-dâi.** |
| | ฉัน ส่งอีเมล์ ไม่ได้ |
| | [MALE] **Phŏm sòng ii-meo mâi-dâi.** |
| | ผม ส่งอีเมล์ ไม่ได้ |
| **Where can I find an Internet café?** | **Ráan-In-ter-nèt yòu thîi-năi?** |
| | ร้านอินเตอร์เน็ตอยู่ที่ไหน |
| **What is the hourly rate to use the Internet?** | **Chái In-ter-nèt chûa-mohng thâo-rài?** |
| | ใช้อินเตอร์เน็ตชั่วโมง เท่าไร |
| **My laptop's battery is out of power.** | [FEMALE] **Nóht-búk khăawng chăn bàaet mòt.** |
| | โน้ตบุ๊ค ของฉัน แบต หมด |
| | [MALE] **Cawm-phíew-têr khăawng phŏm bàaet mòt.** |
| | คอมพิวเตอร์ ของผม แบตหมด |

**Nóht-búk** or "computer notebook" can also mean laptops. Thais use **bàaet** which is adopted from "battery" to refer to computer batteries in English.

| | |
|---|---|
| **Can I charge my laptop here?** | **Khăaw cháat nóht-búk thîi nîi dâi-mái?** |
| | ขอชาร์จ โน้ตบุ๊ค ที่นี่ ได้ไหม |

**Cháat** is borrowed from "to charge a battery" in English. It can also be used for charging a cellphone battery. You can say **muue-thǔue** (or "cellphone") to replace "laptop" in the sentence. For example, **Khǎaw cháat muue-thǔue thîi nîi dâi-mái?** "Can I charge my cell phone here?"

| **Do you have a charger?** | **Khun mii sǎay cháat mái?** |
| | คุณมีสายชาร์จไหม |

**Sǎay cháat** means a charger.

| **My laptop is spoilt.** | [FEMALE] **Nóht-búk khǎawng chǎn sǐa.** |
| | โน้ตบุ๊ค ของฉัน เสีย |
| | [MALE] **Cawm-phíew-têr khǎawng phǒm sǐa.** |
| | คอมพิวเตอร์ ของผม เสีย |

Thais love chatting and using social media to keep up with friends. The four most popular social network apps are Line, Facebook, Instagram, and Twitter. (Data has been taken from a report by Thoth Zocial, a Thai analytics firm.)

**Facebook** Fét-búk เฟซบุ๊ก
Thailand ranks eighth in the world in the number of Facebook users and third in Southeast Asia. As of mid-May 2016, Thailand had 41 million Facebook users out of the 1.79 billion active users worldwide.

**LINE** Laai ไลน์
LINE is by far the most popular messenger app in Thailand, mainly because you can send cute "stickers" with

funny wordings to express emotions and some Thais often spend money to purchase new sets of stickers. LINE was one of the first apps to introduce free calls—deducted from the data usage allowance you have—as well as voice messages (which has become more and more popular).

### Instagram In-sà-taa-graem อินสตาแกรม
In 2016, Instagram reached over 500 million users, of which 7.8 million users are Thai people. Thais love taking pictures of the marvelous architecture and scenic views in their country, but more commonly, documenting their lives, food, pets, and taking loads of selfies.

### Twitter Thá-wít-têr ทวิตเตอร์
Twitter is one of the important social networks with a huge impact on Thai culture. These days, busy people who do not have time to watch TV or read the newspaper prefer to use Twitter to keep themselves up to date. There are now 5.3 million Thai people on Twitter who average 5.5 tweets per day.

### YouTube You-thóup ยูทูป
There are 16 million YouTube users in Thailand. Thailand has moved up to the top ten countries in the world who spend the most time watching YouTube videos (about 1.7 hours per day), according to a recent announcement from Google Thailand, of which most are 18 to 45-year-olds.

### WhatsApp Wáwt-áep วอทซ์แอพ

### FaceTime Fét-thaam เฟซไทม์

**WeChat** Wii-cháet วีแชท

**SnapChat** Sà-náep-cháet สแนปแชท

**Blog** Bláwk บล็อก

**to upload** Áp-lòht อัพโหลด

| | |
|---|---|
| **I'll upload these pictures on my Facebook.** | [FEMALE] **Chǎn jà áp-lòht rôup long Fét-búk.** ฉัน จะอัพโหลดรูปลงเฟซบุ๊ก |
| | [MALE] **Phǒm jà áp-lòht rôup long Fét-búk.** ผม จะอัพโหลดรูปลงเฟซบุ๊ก |
| **App/application** | **Áep** แอพ |
| **This app is really good.** | **Áep níi dii mâak loey.** แอพนี้ดีมากเลย |
| **This app kinda sucks.** | **Áep níi yâe mâak.** แอพนี้แย่มาก |

Having some of these apps can help you instantly start a conversation.

**Games:** Hay Day, Jelly Blast, Cookie Run, QuizClash, Candy Crush Saga

**Photography:** Camera360, FotoRus, BeautyPlus, B612, Boomerang, Snow

**Beauty:** Perfect365, Beauty Camera, Selfie Kamera

**Currency exchange:** XE Currency, SuperRich, Thai Exchange, Exchange TH 2

**Hotel booking:** Airbnb, Booking.com, Agoda, Hotels Thailand, Trivago, Hotels.com

**Public transport:** Bangkok Transport, Bangkok Metro Map, Bangkok Transit, Grab, Uber

| | |
|---|---|
| **Do you have a Facebook account?** | **Khun mii Fét-búk mái?**<br>คุณมี เฟซบุ๊ค หม |
| **Can I add you (as a friend) on Facebook?** | [FEMALE] **Chǎn áaet khun pen phûean dâi-mái?**<br>ฉัน แอดคุณเป็น เพื่อนได้ไหม<br>[MALE] **Phǒm áaet khun pen phûean dâi-mái?**<br>ผม แอดคุณเป็น เพื่อนได้ไหม |
| **Do you have a Instagram account?** | **Khun mii In-sà-taa-graem mái?**<br>คุณมี อินสตาแกรมไ หม |
| **Do you have a Line account?** | **Khun mii Laai mái?**<br>คุณมีไลน์ไหม |
| **Can I have your Line user ID?** | **Khǎaw ai-dii Laai khǎawng khun dâi-mái?**<br>ขอไอดีไลน์ของคุณได้ไหม |

| **What kind of cellphone do you have?** | **Khun chái muue-thǔue rûn nǎi?** |
| | คุณใช้มือถือรุ่นไหน |

**Muue-thǔue** ("cellphone") can be simply used to refer to "smart phones" as well.

| **I've got (a/an)...** | [FEMALE] **Chǎn chái...** |
| | ฉัน ใช้... |
| | [MALE] **Phǒm chái...** |
| | ผม ใช้... |

| **iPhone** | **Ai-fohn** ไอโฟน |
| **Samsung** | **Sam-sung** ซัมซุง |
| **Asus** | **Ay-sút** เอ-ซุส |
| **Huawei** | **Hǔa-wòei** หัวเหว่ย |
| **Oppo** | **Órp-pôh** ออปโป |
| **Sony** | **Soh-nîi** โซนี่ |
| **LG** | **Ael-jii** แอลจี |
| **Vivo** | **Wii-wôh** วีโว่ |

**Berr** is shortened from "number" in English.

| **Will you text me?** | [FEMALE] **Sòng khâw-khwaam hǎa chǎn dâi-mái?** |
| | ส่งข้อความ หาฉัน ได้ไหม |

| **Will you SMS me?** | [MALE] **Sòng SMS hǎa phǒm dâi-mái?** |
| | ส่งSMS หาผม ได้ไหม |

| I'll send you the picture via Line. | **Chăn jà sòng thaang Laai.**<br>ฉัน จะส่งทาง ไลน์ |
| I'll send you the picture via Whatsapp. | **Phŏm jà sòng thaang Wáwt-áep.**<br>ผม จะส่งทาง วอทซ์แอพ |
| I don't understand how to use this, will you teach me? | [FEMALE] **Chăn mâi róu wâa tham yang-ngai, khun săawn dâi-mái?**<br>ฉัน ไม่รู้ว่าทำยังไง คุณ สอนได้ไหม<br>[MALE] **Phŏm mâi róu wâa tham yang-ngai, khun săawn dâi-mái?**<br>ผมไม่รู้ว่าทำยังไง คุณ สอนได้ไหม |

## DATING APPLICATIONS

You can also use some of these apps to meet people during your stay in Thailand.

**Tinder**

Tinder is a popular dating app where the user swipes right on the pictures of their potential matches, if they like what they see, or to the left if they don't. Like other major cities in the world, Tinder has a following in some cities of Thailand, especially in Bangkok. Tinder is particularly popular with young people searching for other young people but can also used by travelers and expats.

**Beetalk**

It is an application for chatting with friends and dates in the vicinity by using the smartphone's GPS as well as your own contacts, so you can chat with your friends and meet potential dates who work or live near you.

## UNDERSTANDING THAI TEXTSPEAK

Originally used when chatting with people on instant messaging sites like ICQ or MSN Messenger, textspeak or chatspeak—texting shorthand, with different spelling and tone marks from the standard Thai and abbreviated English loanwords—is now used also on social networking apps on smartphones. While the lexicon is always evolving, here are some examples of the most popular Thai textspeak.

**555 hâa hâa hâa**
It is a special Thai version of LOL ("laugh out loud") and is used as substitutes for laughter. You can type more than three 5's depending on how funny you think the conversation is (or how hard you're "laughing").

**O โอ / Khay เค / Khray เคร / O-chay โอเช**
These are alternative forms of saying "Okay/OK".

**Dii jâa ดีจ้า**
It is a very informal chatspeak for saying "Hello" in Thai. It should be used with friends or someone you know very well.

**Bai บัย**
It is adapted and shortened from "goodbye" in English.

**Brâa** บร้า
It is used as a slang to mean "crazy", "weird" or "silly", but it doesn't have a negative meaning.

**Răa** หรา
It means "Really?" and is used to express doubt like "I don't believe you" in a sarcastic and humorous way. Sometimes people use drawn-out vowels such as **"răaaaa"** to make the word sound even more sarcastic.

**Júp júp** จุ๊บจุ๊บ
It is used for expressing "kisses" or as an alternative to "xoxo" (hugs and kisses)

# 8

# Getting Social

Thais are very friendly, and most of the young people are okay with talking to foreigners, although they can only speak a little English. Use the phrases and expressions in this section to strike up a conversation with a Thai person, which should help you start chatting, change the topic, continue and end the conversation in Thai.

| | |
|---|---|
| **Excuse me.** | **Khǎaw thôht.** ขอโทษ |
| **Is this seat taken?** (Is someone sitting here?) | **Trong níi mii khon nâng mái?** ตรงนี้มีคนนั่งไหม |
| **Do you mind if I join you?** | **Khǎaw nâng dûay dâi mái?** ขอนั่งด้วยได้ไหม |
| **Do you want to sit down?** | **Nâng dûay gan mái?** นั่งด้วยกันไหม |

| | |
|---|---|
| **What are you drinking?** | **Khun dùuem à-rai?**<br>คุณ ดื่ม อะไร |
| **What are you eating?** | **Khun gin à-rai?**<br>คุณ กิน อะไร |
| **Do you come here often?** | **Khun maa thîi nîi bòy mái?**<br>คุณมาที่นี่บ่อยไหม |
| **How do you know of this place?** | **Khun róu-jàk thîi nîi dâi yang-ngai?**<br>คุณรู้จักที่นี่ได้ยังไง |
| **I heard (about it) from my friends.** | **Jàak phûean.** จากเพื่อน |
| **Do you know what time this place closes?** | **Khun róu mái thîi nîi pìt gìi mohng?**<br>คุณรู้ไหมที่นี่ปิดกี่โมง |

This question literally means, "Are you originally from here?" You can also use a name of the city, province or district that you are in at the moment to replace "here" in the sentence, for e.g., **Khun pen khon Chiang-mài rúe plào?** (Are you from Chiang Mai?)

| | |
|---|---|
| **My name is...** | [FEMALE] **Chăn chúue...**<br>ฉัน ชื่อ... |
| | [MALE] **Phŏm chúue...**<br>ผม ชื่อ... |
| **What's your name?** | **Khun chúue à-rai?**<br>คุณชื่ออะไร |

| How long have you been here? | **Khun yòu thîi nîi naan rúe yang?** คุณอยู่ที่นี่นานหรือยัง |
|---|---|
| Where do you live? | **Bâan khǎawng khun yòu thîi-nǎi?** บ้านของคุณอยู่ที่ไหน? |
| Where are you from? | **Khun maa jàak thîi-nǎi?** คุณมาจากที่ไหน |
| Do you live in this city? | **Khun pen khon thîi nîi rúe plào?** คุณเป็นคนที่นี่รึเปล่า |
| I'm from America, now I live in Bangkok. | [FEMALE] **Chǎn maa jàak À-may-rí-gaa, tawn níi yòu thîi mueang Grung-thêp.** ฉัน มาจากประเทศ อเมริกา ตอนนี้อยู่เมือง กรุงเทพฯ [MALE] **Phǒm maa jàak À-may-rí-gaa, tawn níi yòu thîi mueang Grung-thêp.** ผม มาจากประเทศ อเมริกา ตอนนี้อยู่เมือง กรุงเทพฯ |

More countries and nationalities in the English-Thai dictionary (page 134 onwards)

| Have you ever lived in another country? | **Khun khoey yòu tàang prà-thêt rúe plào?** คุณเคยอยู่ต่างประเทศ หรือเปล่า |
|---|---|

**What languages do you know how to speak?**

Khun phôut phaa-sǎa à-rai dâi bâang?
คุณพูดภาษาอะไรได้บ้าง

**Your English is good.**

Khun phôut phaa-sǎa ang-grìt gèng mâak.
คุณพูดภาษาอังกฤษเก่ง

**How old are you?**

Khun aa-yú gìi pii?
คุณอายุกี่ปี?

**What's your job?**

Khun tham-ngaan à-rai?
คุณทำงานอะไร?

**I work with computers.**

[MALE] Phǒm tham-ngaan dâan cawm-phíew-têr.
ผม ทำงานด้าน คอมพิวเตอร

**I'm a lawyer.**

[FEMALE] Chǎn pen Thá-naay-khwaam.
ฉัน เป็น ทนายความ

**I'm a/an...**

[FEMALE] Chǎn pen...
ฉัน เป็น...
[MALE] Phǒm pen...
ผม เป็น...

| | |
|---|---|
| **office worker** | phá-nák-ngaan baaw-rí-sàt พนักงานบริษัท |
| **business person** | nák-thú-rá-gìt นักธุรกิจ |
| **engineer** | wít-sà-wá-gawn วิศวกร |

| | |
|---|---|
| **mechanic** | **châang** ช่าง |
| **doctor** | **mǎaw** หมอ |
| **lawyer** | **thá-naay-khwaam** ทนายความ |
| **police officer** | **tam-rùat** ตำรวจ |
| **salesperson** | **phá-nák-ngaan-khǎai** พนักงานขาย |
| **military person** | **thá-hǎan** ทหาร |
| **government official** | **khâa-râat-chá-gaan** ข้าราชการ |
| **teacher/instructor** | **khrou** ครู |
| **hairstylist** | **châang-tham-phǒm** ช่างทำผม |
| **university student** | **nák-sùek-sǎa** นักศึกษา |

| | |
|---|---|
| **Where are you studying?** | **Khun rian thîi-nǎi?** คุณเรียนที่ไหน |
| **At which university?** | **Má-hǎa-wít-thá-yaa-lai à-rai?** มหาวิทยาลัยอะไร |
| **I go to ... university/college.** | [FEMALE] **Chǎn rian thîi má-hǎa-wít-thá-yaa-lai...** ฉันเรียนที่ มหาวิทยาลัย...<br>[MALE] **Phǒm rian thîi má-hǎa-wít-thá-yaa-lai...** ผมเรียนที่ มหาวิทยาลัย... |

| When I was a student, I... | [FEMALE] **Tawn pen nák-sùek-săa, chăn...** ตอนเป็นนักศึกษา ฉัน... |
| | [MALE] **Tawn pen nák-sùek-săa, phŏm...** ตอนเป็นนักศึกษา ผม... |

| | |
|---|---|
| **played in a band** | **lên don-trii** เล่นดนตรี |
| **played soccer** | **lên fùt-baawn** เล่นฟุตบอล |
| **played American football** | **lên à-me-rí-gan fùt-baawn** เล่นอเมริกันฟุตบอล |
| **played basketball** | **lên báat-sà-gêt-baawn** บาสเกตบอล |
| **was on the swim team** | **pen nák-wâay-náam** เป็นนักว่ายน้ำ |
| **was on the track team** | **pen nák-wîng** เป็นนักวิ่ง |

| I like ... during my free time. | [FEMALE] **Way-laa-wâang chăn châawp...** เวลาว่าง ฉันชอบ... |
| | [MALE] **Way-laa-wâang phŏm châawp...** เวลาว่าง ผมชอบ... |

| | |
|---|---|
| **(singing) Karaoke** | **ráawng khaa-raa-oh-gè** ร้องคาราโอเกะ |
| **surfing** | **lên sérp** เล่นเซิร์ฟ |
| **golf** | **lên gáawf** เล่นกอล์ฟ |

| | |
|---|---|
| cycling | **khìi-jàk-grà-yaan** ขี่จักรยาน |
| shopping | **cháawp-pîng** ช้อปปิ้ง |
| working on my car | **tàaeng rót** แต่งรถ |
| going to concerts | **dou khawn-sèrt** ดูคอนเสิร์ต |
| playing guitar | **lên gii-tâa** เล่นกีตาร์ |
| playing drums | **lên tii-glawng** เล่ตีกลอง |
| playing drums | **lên pia-noh** เล่นเปียโน |
| playing video games | **lên wii-dii-oh game** เล่นวิดีโอเกมส์ |

| | |
|---|---|
| **How long have you been in Thailand?** | **Khun yòu prà-thêt Thai naan thâo-rài láew?** คุณอยู่ประเทศไทยนาน เท่าไรแล้ว |
| **I've lived in Thailand for … months.** | [FEMALE] **Chǎn yòu prà-thêt Thai … duean.** ฉัน อยู่ประเทศไทย… เดือน |
| **I've lived in Thailand for … years.** | [MALE] **Phǒm yòu prà-thêt Thai … pii.** ผม อยู่ประเทศไทย…ปี |
| **I'm not shy.** | [FEMALE] **Chǎn mâi khîi aai.** ฉัน ไม่ขี้อาย |
| | [MALE] **Phǒm mâi khîi aai.** ผม ไม่ขี้อาย |

| | |
|---|---|
| **Do you mind if I smoke?** | [FEMALE] **Chǎn sòup-bù-rìi dâi-mái?**<br>ฉัน สูบบุหรี่ได้ไหม<br>[MALE] **Phǒm sòup-bù-rìi dâi-mái?**<br>ผม สูบบุหรี่ได้ไหม |

If you want to keep the conversation going—and the person you're talking to seems receptive to it—you can follow up with these questions.

| | |
|---|---|
| **What do you usually do on weekends?** | **Wan yùt khun châawp tham à-rai?**<br>วันหยุดคุณชอบทำอะไร |
| **How often do you go out?** | **Khun àawk pai-thîaw bòy mái?**<br>คุณออกไปเที่ยวบ่อยไหม |
| **Where do you like to go?** | **Khun châawp pai-thîaw thîi-nǎi?**<br>คุณชอบไปเที่ยวที่ไหน |
| **What do you usually do with your friends?** | **Khun gàp phûean châawp tham à-rai?**<br>คุณกับเพื่อนชอบทำอะไร |
| **Do you like pets?** | **Khun mii sàt líang mái?**<br>คุณมีสัตว์เลี้ยงไหม |
| **Do you have any?** | **Khun líang à-rai?**<br>คุณเลี้ยงอะไร |

| | |
|---|---|
| **I have (a)...** | [FEMALE] **Chăn líang...** ฉัน เลี้ยง... |
| | [MALE] **Phŏm líang...** ผม เลี้ยง... |

| | |
|---|---|
| **Dog** | **Măa** หมา |
| **Cat** | **Maaew** แมว |
| **Bird** | **Nók** นก |
| **Hamster** | **Nŏu haaem-sà-têr** หนูแฮมสเตอร์ |
| **Rabbit** | **Grà-tàay** กระต่าย |
| **Goldfish** | **Plaa-thawng** ปลาทอง |
| **Turtle** | **Tào** เต่า |
| **Parrot** | **Nók-gâaew** นกแก้ว |
| **Horse** | **Máa** ม้า |

| | |
|---|---|
| **Do you like to cook?** | **Khun châawp tham-aa-hăan mái?** คุณชอบทำอาหารไหม |
| **What is your favorite food?** | **Khun châawp gin à-rai?** คุณชอบกินอะไร |
| **My favorite food is...** | [FEMALE] **Chăn châawp gin...** ฉัน ชอบกิน... |
| | [MALE] **Phŏm châawp gin...** ผม ชอบกิน... |

| | |
|---|---|
| **Pizza** | Pít-sâa พิซซ่า |
| **Steak** | Sà-ték สเต็ก |
| **Salad** | Sà-làt สลัด |
| **Pasta** | Páat-sà-tâa พาสต้า |
| **Noodles** | Gǔay-tǐaw ก๋วยเตี๋ยว |
| **Burger** | Berr-gêr เบอร์เกอร์ |
| **French fries** | Frén-fraay เฟรนช์ฟรายด์ |
| **Fried chicken** | Gài-thâawt ไก่ทอด |
| **Tacos** | Thaa-gôh ทาโก้ |
| **Sushi** | Sou-shí ซูช |
| **Lasagna** | Laa-saan-yâa ลาซานญ่า |
| **Hot dogs** | Háawt-dàawk ฮ็อทดอก |

| | |
|---|---|
| **Do you play any sport?** | Khun châawp lên gii-laa mái? คุณชอบเล่นกีฬาไหม |
| **(If so) what sport do you play?** | Khun châawp lên gii-laa à-rai? คุณชอบเล่นกีฬาอะไร |
| **I like to play…** | [FEMALE] Chǎn lên… ฉัน ชอบเล่น… [MALE] Phǒm lên… ผม ชอบเล่น… |

| | |
|---|---|
| **Tennis** | Ten-nít เทนนิส |
| **Golf** | Gáawf กอล์ฟ |
| **Bowling** | Boh-lîng โบว์ลิ่ง |
| **Badminton** | Bàaet-min-tân แบดมินตัน |
| **Table tennis** | Ping-paawng ปิงปอง |
| **Soccer/football** | Fút-baawn ฟุตบอล |
| **Basketball** | Báat-sà-gét-baawn บาสเก็ตบอล |
| **Volleyball** | Waawn-lây-baawn วอลเลย์บอล |
| **Squash** | Sà-khwáwt สควอช |
| **Rugby** | Rák-bîi รักบี้ |
| **American football** | À-may-rí-gan fút-baawn อเมริกันฟุตบอล |
| **Baseball** | Bés-baawn เบสบอล |

| | |
|---|---|
| **I like...** | [FEMALE] Chǎn châawp... ฉัน ชอบ... |
| | [MALE] Phǒm châawp... ผม ชอบ... |

| | |
|---|---|
| **Running** | Wîng วิ่ง |
| **Swimming** | Wâay-náam ว่ายน้ำ |
| **Sailing** | Ruea-bai เรือใบ |

| | |
|---|---|
| **Cycling** | **Pàn-jàk-grà-yaan** ปั่นจักรยาน |
| **Windsurfing** | **Win-sérp** วินด์เซิร์ฟ |
| **Rock climbing** | **Piin-nâa-phǎa** ปีนหน้าผา |

| | |
|---|---|
| **This is a great song.** | **Phleng níi phráw.** เพลงนี้เพราะ |
| **Do you know this song?** | **Khun róu jàk phleng níi mái?** คุณรู้จักเพลงนี้ไหม |
| **I know it.** | [FEMALE] **Chǎn róu jàk phleng níi.** ฉัน รู้จักเพลงนี้ |
| **I don't know it.** | [MALE] **Phǒm mâi róu jàk phleng níi.** ผมไม่รู้จักเพลงนี้ |
| **I love pop music.** | [FEMALE] **Chǎn châawp phleng Páwp.** ฉัน ชอบเพลงป๊อบ |
| | [MALE] **Phǒm châawp phleng Páwp.** ผม ชอบเพลงป๊อบ |
| **How about you?** | **Khun châawp mái?** คุณชอบไหม |

| | |
|---|---|
| **I like it.** | [FEMALE] **Chăn châawp.**<br>ฉัน ชอบ<br>[MALE] **Phŏm châawp.**<br>ผม ชอบ |
| **I like it a lot./I love it.** | [FEMALE] **Chăn châawp mâak.**<br>ฉัน ชอบมาก<br>[MALE] **Phŏm châawp mâak.**<br>ผม ชอบมาก |
| **I don't really like it.** | [FEMALE] **Chăn mâi kòy châawp.**<br>ฉัน ไม่ค่อยชอบ<br>[MALE] **Phŏm mâi kòy châawp.**<br>ผม ไม่ค่อยชอบ |
| **Can I buy you a drink?** | [FEMALE, FORMAL] **Chăn khăaw khrûeang-dùuem dâi-mái?**<br>ฉัน ขอเครื่องดื่ม ได้ไหม |
| **Can I buy you a drink?** | [MALE, INFORMAL] **Phŏm khăaw líang náam dâi-mái?**<br>ผม ขอเลี้ยง น้ำ ได้ไหม |

**Krûeang-duuèm** means "beverage" and is mostly used in formal setting, while **náam** (literally: "water") can be used alternatively in informal settings. (Refer to pages 63-65 for the list of drinks that you can order.)

| | |
|---|---|
| **What would you like?** | **Khun yàak dùuem à-rai?**<br>คุณอยาก ดื่ม อะไร |
| **Are you having a good time?** | **Khun sà-nùk mái?**<br>คุณสนุกไหม |

| | |
|---|---|
| **Yeah, I'm having fun.** | **Sà-nùk.** สนุก |
| **No, not really.** | **Mâi khòy sà-nùk.** ไม่ค่อยสนุก |
| **What time are you leaving?** | **Khun jà glàp bâan gìi-mohng?** คุณจะกลับบ้านกี่โมง |
| **I haven't decided.** | [FEMALE] **Chăn yang mâi róu loey.** ฉัน ยังไม่รู้เลย |
| | [MALE] **Phŏm yang mâi róu loey.** ผม ยังไม่รู้เลย |
| **I haven't decided yet.** | [FEMALE] **Chăn yang khít mâi àawk.** ฉัน ยังคิดไม่ออก |
| | [MALE] **Phŏm yang khít mâi àawk.** ผม ยังคิดไม่ออก |
| **Shall we go some-where else** (together)**?** | **Rao pai thîi ùen gan mái?** เราไปที่อื่นกันไหม |

### Staying Safe

It is not advisable to go back to your hostel, guest-house or home with strangers, no matter where you are in the world. Women, especially solo travelers, should be somewhat sober when interacting with the opposite sex, to reduce chances of getting into a bad situation.

Also, be aware that an innocent flirtation might send a wrong signal or intention to a recipient who does not share your culture's sexual norms.

| | |
|---|---|
| **Can my friends come?** | [FEMALE] **Phûean khǎawng chǎn pai dûay dâi mái?** เพื่อน ของฉัน ไปด้วย ได้ไหม? |
| | [MALE] **Phûean khǎawng phǒm pai dûay dâi mái?** เพื่อน ของผม ไปด้วย ได้ไหม? |
| **Shall we leave?** | **Rao pai gan loey mái?** เราไปกันเลยไหม? |
| **What's next?** | **Pai nǎi dii?** ไปไหนดี |
| **Have you decided?** | **Khun khít àwk rúe yang?** คุณคิดออกหรือยัง? |
| **It's up to you.** | **Láaew tàae khun.** แล้วแต่คุณ |
| **Anything's fine.** | **Yang-ngai gâaw dâi.** ยังไงก็ได้ |
| **Anywhere's okay.** | **Thîi-nǎi gâaw dâi.** ที่ไหนก็ได้ |
| **Shall we go shopping?** | **Pai cháawp-pîng gan mái?** ไปช็อปปิ้งกันไหม |

| | |
|---|---|
| **Shall we go bowling?** | **Pai lên boh-lǐng gan mái?** |
| | ไปเล่นโบว์ลิ่งกันไหม |
| **Let's go have lunch.** | **Pai gin khâow thîang gan.** |
| | ไปกิน ข้าวเที่ยง กัน |
| **Let's go have brunch.** | **Pai gin múue sǎay gan.** |
| | ไปกิน มื้อสาย กัน |
| **Let's go have dinner.** | **Pai gin khâow-yen gan.** |
| | ไปกิน ข้าวเย็น กัน |
| **Let's go have dessert.** | **Pai gin khà-nǒm gan.** |
| | ไปกิน ขนม กัน |
| **Let's go see a movie.** | **Pai dou nǎng gan.** |
| | ไปดูหนังกัน |
| **I'd like to stay here longer.** | [FEMALE] **Chǎn yàak yòu tàaw.** |
| | ฉัน อยากอยู่ต่อ |
| | [MALE] **Phǒm yàak yòu tàaw.** |
| | ผม อยากอยู่ต่อ |
| **I'll go home.** | [FEMALE] **Chǎn jà glàp bâan.** |
| | ฉัน จะกลับบ้าน |
| | [MALE] **Phǒm jà glàp bâan.** |
| | ผม จะกลับบ้าน |
| **Shall we meet again?** | **Rao jerr gan ìik dâi mái?** |
| | เราเจอกันอีกได้ไหม? |
| **I really enjoyed talking to you.** | **Khuy gàp khun sà-nùk mâak.** |
| | คุยกับคุณสนุกมาก |

| | |
|---|---|
| **When can I see you again?** | [FEMALE] **Chăn jà jerr khun ìik mûea-rài?** ฉัน จะเจอคุณอีก เมื่อไร [MALE] **Phŏm jà jerr khun ìik mûea-rài?** ผม จะเจอคุณอีก เมื่อไร |
| **May I call you?** | [FEMALE] **Chăn thoh hăa khun dâi mái?** ฉัน โทรหาคุณ ได้ไหม [MALE] **Phŏm thoh hăa khun dâi mái?** ผม โทรหาคุณ ได้ไหม |
| **Thanks a lot.** | **Khàawp-khun mâak.** ขอบคุณมาก |
| **Take care.** | **Thék khaae** เทคแคร์ |
| **Take care.** (Good luck.) | **Chôhk-dii.** โชคดี |

You can either say "Take care" in Thai pronunciation or "**Chôhk-dii**" which literally means "Good luck".

| | |
|---|---|
| **See you later.** | **Láaew jerr gan.** แล้วเจอกัน |
| **See you tomorrow.** | **Jerr gan phrûng níi.** เจอกันพรุ่งนี้ |
| **Bye!** | **Baay!** บาย |

# 9

# Love and Dating

Every culture has a different idea of dating or flirting. The dating culture in Thailand is a bit different than it is in the West, even though in recent years it has become slightly less traditional and Thai women (between age 19-27) often ask men out on a date.

There are a lot of things that you should know about cultural norms that you may not be accustomed to when dating a Thai woman (or man). Here are some good tips for you:

Don't assume all Thai women are hookers. In Thailand, there are generally two sorts of women: normal Thai girls and those you can meet in bars/pubs. While there are many Thai women/men online that are just looking for some short-term fun or one night stands with a Westerner, others may be looking for a serious relationship.

Most Thai girls are conservative so it's better to avoid public displays of affection as it is considered inappropriate. A bit of hand holding outside after you've been on a couple of dates with her is generally acceptable. Some younger Thais may be more open to showing affection.

Instead of going to bars or clubs on your first date, do a bit of research to pick the right place, for example, a dinner date at a nice restaurant along the Chao Praya river in Bangkok. Steer clear of conversation topics like income, age, weight, height, Thai politics, religion and the royal family.

Make sure to be courteous and polite on your date, especially to the wait staff.

Dress nicely. Thais are more sensitive to dress, cleanliness, and appearance than foreigners. For western women dating Thai guys, avoid wearing clothes that are too revealing, especially when meeting his friends and family.

Don't be surprised if a Thai girl brings a few friends or her cousins along on the first date to keep her safe and also to observe your behavior.

Most girls are appreciative if you pay for the first date. Some might insist on paying for their half or at least some because Thai women are becoming more successful and financially independent and they like to show it.

If you get into a serious relationship with a Thai woman or man, you will eventually meet the parents—a clear sign to them that you intend to marry her/him in the future. Be very respectful towards his/her parents and accept a great deal of involvement by them in decision making. Thai children are raised to understand and all of the sacrifices that their parents have made for them throughout their lives, and should show them great respect.

Below are some Thai words and phrases that come in handy for you to communicate with a Thai person.

| | |
|---|---|
| **I want to hang out sometime.** | [FEMALE] **Chăn yàak chuan khun pai thîaw lên.** ฉัน อยากชวนคุณไป เที่ยวเล่น |
| | [MALE] **Phŏm yàak chuan khun pai thîaw lên.** ผม อยากชวนคุณไป เที่ยวเล่น |

**Pai thîaw lên** (ไปเที่ยวเล่น) or "hang out" to Thais means going out to do some activities, such as having a meal, coffee, watching a movie, or (window) shopping at the mall.

The following phrases can be used to check if they are available or seeing anyone.

| | |
|---|---|
| **Do you have a steady boy/girlfriend?** | **Khun mii faaen mái?** คุณมีแฟนไหม |
| **Are you married?** | **Khun tàaeng-ngaan?** คุณ แต่งงาน |
| **Are you engaged?** | **Khun mân rúe-yang?** คุณ หมั้น หรือยัง |
| **Yes, I had one, but we broke up recently.** | [FEMALE] **Chăn khoei mii, tàae lêrrk gan láaew.** ฉัน เคยมีแฟน แต่เลิก กันแล้ว |
| | [MALE] **Phŏm khoei mii, tàae lêrrk gan láaew.** ผม เคยมีแฟน แต่เลิก กันแล้ว |

| | |
|---|---|
| **Are you  currently seeing anyone?** | **Khun khóp krai yòu rúe-plào?** คุณคบใครอยู่หรือเปล่า |
| **You must be very popular.** | **Tâawng mii khon jìip khun yér nâae loey.** ต้องมีคนจีบคุณเยอะ แน่เลย |

This phrase literally means "There must be a lot of people hitting on you."

| | |
|---|---|
| **I've never been out on a date with a Thai person.** | [FEMALE] **Chǎn mâi khoey dèt gàp khon thai.** ฉัน ไม่เคยเดทกับ คนไทย |
| | [MALE] **Phǒm mâi khoey dèt gàp khon thai.** ผม ไม่เคยเดทกับ คนไทย |

**Dèt** is adopted from "date" in English with the same meaning. Try these phrases to ask someone out on a date.

| | |
|---|---|
| **What are you doing this weekend?** | **Wan yùt níi khun wâang mái?** วันหยุดนี้คุณว่างไหม |
| **What are you up to this Sunday?** | **Wan aa-thít khun tham à-rai rúe-plào?** วันอาทิตย์คุณทำอะไร หรือเปล่า |
| **Are you free this evening?** | **Yen níi khun wâang mái?** เย็นนี้คุณว่างไหม |

| | |
|---|---|
| **Can we meet tomorrow?** | **Rao jerr gan phrûng-níi dâi-mái?** เราเจอกันพรุ่งนี้ได้ไหม |
| **I was wondering if you'd like to go out?** | **Pai thîaw gan mái?** ไปเที่ยวกันไหม |

Here are some ideas for your date.

Cruising along the Chao Phraya River

Riding on a tuk-tuk together to explore the city

Visiting temples or historical sites, e.g., the Grand Palace Complex, The Temple of the Emerald Buddha, Ayutthaya historical park

Visiting the Chinese temple, trying Chinese food, and buying Chinese products at Chinatown

Having a romantic dinner on a hotel rooftop, such as Baiyoke Tower

Exploring a local market and tasting street food

Watching a movie at a luxury cinema with "VIP seats/ Love seats".

Getting a Thai traditional massage at a nice spa

Visiting famous zoos and animal parks (like Dusit Zoo or Khao Kheow Open Air Zoo) to see an amazing range of animals as well as many activities provided, such as monkey, crocodile, elephant or tiger shows.

| | |
|---|---|
| **Would you like to go for dinner?** | **Pai gin-khâow gan mái?** ไปกินข้าวกันไหม |
| **Could I take you to see a movie?** | **Pai dou-nǎng gan mái?** ไปดูหนังกันไหม |

| | |
|---|---|
| **What would you like to do?** | **Khun yàak tham à-rai?** คุณอยากทำอะไร |
| **What sounds good?** | **Tham à-rai dii?** ทำอะไรดี |
| **Where should we go?** | **Pai năi dii?** ไปไหนดี |
| **Would you like to meet (me) again?** | **Rao jà dâi jerr gan ìik mái?** เราจะได้เจอกันอีกไหม |
| **When can I see you again?** | [FEMALE] **Chăn jà dâi jerr khun ìik mûea-rài?** ฉัน จะได้เจอคุณอีก เมื่อไร<br><br>[MALE] **Phŏm jà dâi jerr khun ìik mûea-rài?** ผม จะได้เจอคุณอีก เมื่อไร |
| **You have a beautiful smile.** | **Khun yìm sŭay.** คุณยิ้มสวย |
| **You are cute.** | **Khun nâa-rák.** คุณน่ารัก |

**Nâa-rák** can be used to describe both appearance and personality.

| | |
|---|---|
| **You're attractive.** | **Khun mii sà-này.** คุณมีเสน่ห์ |
| **You're sexy!** | **Khun dou sék-sîi!** คุณดูเซ็กซี่ |

**Sék-sîi** is a loanword from "sexy" in English.

| | |
|---|---|
| **You're gorgeous!** | **Khun làaw mâak!** |
| (referring to men) | คุณหล่อมาก |
| (referring to women) | **Khun sǔay mâak!** |
| | คุณสวยมาก |

**Làaw** means "handsome", whereas **sǔay** means "beautiful" and it can also be used to talk about general objects and views.

| | |
|---|---|
| **You have beautiful eyes.** | **Taa khun sǔay.** ตาคุณสวย |

| | |
|---|---|
| **Sweet dreams.** | **Fǎn dii.** ฝันดี |

| | |
|---|---|
| **Don't forget to dream about me.** | [FEMALE] **Fǎn thǔeng chǎn dûay ná.** |
| | ฝันถึง ฉัน ด้วยนะ |
| | [MALE] **Fǎn thǔeng phǒm dûay ná.** |
| | ฝันถึง ผม ด้วยนะ |

| | |
|---|---|
| **I think of you night and day.** | [FEMALE] **Chǎn khít-thǔeng khun thúk wan.** |
| | ฉัน คิดถึงคุณทุกวัน |
| | [MALE] **Phǒm khít-thǔeng khun thúk wan.** |
| | ฉัน คิดถึงคุณทุกวัน |

| | |
|---|---|
| **I can't think of anything but you.** | [FEMALE] **Chǎn khít-thǔeng tàae khun.** |
| | ฉัน คิดถึงแต่คุณ |
| | [MALE] **Phǒm khít-thǔeng tàae khun.** |
| | ผม คิดถึงแต่คุณ |

| | |
|---|---|
| **You're special (to me).** | **Khun pen khon phí-sèt.**<br>คุณเป็นคนพิเศษ |
| **I've never felt this way before.** | [FEMALE] **Chǎn mâi khoey róu-sùek bàep níi maa gàwn.**<br>ฉัน ไม่เคยรู้สึกแบบ<br>นี้มาก่อน<br>[MALE] **Phǒm mâi khoey róu-sùek bàep níi maa gàwn.**<br>ผม ไม่เคยรู้สึกแบบนี้<br>มาก่อน |
| **I liked you from the moment I saw you.** | [FEMALE] **Chǎn châawp khun tâng-tàae jerr gan khráng-râaek.**<br>ฉัน ชอบคุณ<br>ตั้งแต่เจอกันครั้งแรก<br>[MALE] **Phǒm châawp khun tâng-tàae jerr gan khráng-râaek.**<br>ผม ชอบคุณ<br>ตั้งแต่เจอกันครั้งแรก |
| **I'm really excited right now.** | [FEMALE] **Chǎn tùuen-tên mâak.**<br>ฉัน ตื่นเต้นมาก |
| **I'm really nervous right now.** | [MALE] **Phǒm tùuen-tên mâak.**<br>ผม ตื่นเต้นมาก |

| | |
|---|---|
| **I'm so happy right now.** | [FEMALE] **Chǎn mii khwâam-sùk mâak.**<br>ฉัน มีความสุขมาก<br>[MALE] **Phǒm mii khwâam-sùk mâak.**<br>ผม มีความสุขมาก |
| **I really like you.** | [FEMALE] **Chǎn châawp khun mâak.** ฉัน ชอบคุณมาก<br>[MALE] **Phǒm châawp khun mâak.** ผม ชอบคุณมาก |
| **I love you.** | [FEMALE] **Chǎn rák khun.**<br>ฉัน รักคุณ<br>[MALE] **Phǒm rák khun.**<br>ผม รักคุณ |
| **You're the only one I love.** | [FEMALE] **Chǎn rák khun khon diaw.**<br>ฉัน รักคุณคนเดียว<br>[MALE] **Phǒm rák khun khon diaw.**<br>ผม รักคุณคนเดียว |
| **I want to stay with you forever.** | [FEMALE] **Chǎn yàak yòu gàp khun tà-lǎawt-pai.**<br>ผม อยากอยู่กับคุณ ตลอดไป<br>[MALE] **Phǒm yàak yòu gàp khun tà-lǎawt-pai.**<br>ผม อยากอยู่กับคุณ ตลอดไป |

| | |
|---|---|
| **Will you marry me?** | [FEMALE] **Tàaeng-ngaan gàp chǎn mái?**<br>แต่งงานกับ ฉัน ไหม<br>[MALE] **Tàaeng-ngaan gàp phǒm mái?**<br>แต่งงานกับ ผม ไหม |

If you aren't ready for marriage, you may need the following responses.

| | |
|---|---|
| **I don't want to get married yet.** | [FEMALE] **Chǎn yang mâi yàak tàaeng-ngaan.**<br>ฉัน ยังไม่อยากแต่งงาน<br>[MALE] **Phǒm yang mâi yàak tàaeng-ngaan.**<br>ผม ยังไม่อยากแต่งงาน |
| **I don't want to get engaged yet.** | [FEMALE] **Chǎn yang mâi yàak mân.**<br>ฉัน ยังไม่อยากหมั้น<br>[MALE] **Phǒm yang mâi yàak mân.**<br>ผม ยังไม่อยากหมั้น |
| **I don't want to think about marriage yet.** | [FEMALE] **Chǎn yang mâi khít rûeang tàaeng-ngaan.**<br>ฉัน ยังไม่คิดเรื่อง แต่งงาน<br>[MALE] **Phǒm yang mâi khít rûeang tàaeng-ngaan.**<br>ผม ยังไม่คิดเรื่อง แต่งงาน |

| | |
|---|---|
| **I love you but I can't marry you.** | [FEMALE] **Chăn rák khun tàe tàaeng-ngaan gàp khun mâi-dâi.** ฉัน รักคุณแต่แต่งงานกับคุณไม่ได้ |
| | [MALE] **Phŏm rák khun tàe tàaeng-ngaan gàp khun mâi-dâi.** ผม รักคุณแต่แต่งงานกับคุณไม่ได้ |
| **Don't get me wrong.** | [FEMALE] **Yàa khâo-jai chăn phìt.** อย่าเข้าใจ ฉัน ผิด |
| **You are a wonderful guy.** | **Khun pen khon dii mâak.** คุณเป็นคนดีมาก |
| **I'm not good for you.** | [FEMALE] **Chăn mâi dii phaaw.** ฉัน ไม่ดีพอ |
| | [MALE] **Phŏm mâi dii phaaw.** ผม ไม่ดีพอ |

Chastity, especially for the Thai woman, has been long held in high regard, so intimacy is unlikely to happen outside marriage and definitely not within the first few dates. If it does, it's likely the woman expects the relationship to lead to marriage, so you may want to be cautious about this. Here are some phrases you can use when doing the deed:

| | |
|---|---|
| **May I kiss you?** | **Khăaw jòup dâi-mái?** ขอจูบได้ไหม |

| | |
|---|---|
| **Be with me tonight.** | [FEMALE] **Khuuen níi yòu gàp chǎn ná.** คืนนี้อยู่กับ ฉัน นะ |
| | [MALE] **Khuuen níi yòu gàp phǒm ná.** คืนนี้อยู่กับ ผม นะ |
| **You smell good.** | **Khun tua hǎwm jang.** คุณตัวหอมจัง |

**Jang** is commonly used to mean "so much", "extremely", or "greatly", and placed behind an adjective to give the emphasis.

| | |
|---|---|
| **You have a beautiful body.** | **Khun rôup-râang-sǔay/ hùn-dii jang.** คุณ รูปร่างสวย/หุ่นดี จัง |
| **I'm embarrassed.** | [FEMALE] **Chǎn aay.** ฉัน อาย |
| | [MALE] **Phǒm aay.** ผม อาย |
| **Don't be shy.** | **Mâi tâawng aai.** ไม่ต้องอาย |
| **Close your eyes.** | **Làp taa sì.** หลับตาสิ |
| **Did you like (that)?** | **Khun châawp mái?** คุณชอบไหม |
| **That was good.** | **Dii jang.** ดีจัง |
| **Your lips are so soft.** | **Pàak khun nûm mâak.** ปากคุณนุ่มมาก |

| | |
|---|---|
| **I like kissing you.** | [FEMALE] **Chăn châawp jòup khun.** ฉัน ชอบจูบคุณ |
| | [MALE] **Phŏm châawp jòup khun.** ผม ชอบจูบคุณ |
| **Hold me tight.** | [FEMALE] **Gàawt chăn nâaen nâaen.** กอดฉันแน่นๆ |
| | [MALE] **Gàawt phŏm nâaen nâaen.** กอดผมแน่นๆ |

In Thai, you say the same word twice in order to emphasize it; **nâaen nâaen** literally means "tight tight".

Sometimes, you may experience some conflict in your relationship. Use these phrases to express your frustration.

| | |
|---|---|
| **What do you want?** | **Khun jà ao yang-ngai?** คุณจะเอายังไง |
| **What did you say?** | **Khun phôut à-rai ná?** คุณพูดอะไรนะ |
| **Why do you talk like that?** | **Tham-mai khun phôut bàaep nán.** ทำไมคุณพูดแบบนั้น |
| **I'm bored.** | [MALE] **Phŏm bùea.** ผมเบื่อ |
| **I'm upset.** | [FEMALE] **Chăn seng.** ฉันเซ็ง |

**Seng** is a slang meaning "upset".

| | |
|---|---|
| **That's stupid!** | **Rái săa-rá!** ไร้สาระ |
| **Stop it.** | **Phaaw thèr.** พอเถอะ |

| | |
|---|---|
| **Don't joke around with me!** | [FEMALE] **Yàa maa phôut lên gàp chǎn!** อย่ามาพูดเล่นกับฉัน [MALE] **Yàa maa phôut lên gàp phǒm!** อย่ามาพูดเล่นกับผม |

This phrase is used when someone is acting stupidly or has said something stupid.

| | |
|---|---|
| **It's not funny.** | **Mâi tà-lòk ná.** ไม่ตลกนะ |
| **Liar!** | **Khon goh-hòk!** คนโกหก |
| **You've got a big mouth!** | **Khun phôut mâak!** คุณพูดมาก |

Use this for someone who's always spreading the latest rumors, people's secrets, etc.

| | |
|---|---|
| **That's a lie!** | **Goh-hòk!** โกหก |
| **Don't lie!** | **Yàa goh-hòk!** อย่าโกหก |
| **Don't do that!** | **Yàa tham yàang nán!** อย่าทำอย่างนั้น |
| **Why do you do things like that?** | **Tham-mai khun tham yàang nán?** ทำไมคุณทำอย่างนั้น |
| **You're being annoying!** | **Khun nâa ram-khaan!** คุณน่ารำคาญ |

| | |
|---|---|
| **I'm going to leave now.** | [FEMALE] **Chăn jà glàp láaew ná.** ฉัน จะกลับแล้วนะ |
| | [MALE] **Phŏm jà glàp láaew ná.** ผม จะกลับแล้วนะ |
| **Leave me alone!** | [FEMALE] **Yàa maa yûng gàp chăn!** อย่ามายุ่งกับฉัน |
| | [MALE] **Yàa maa yûng gàp phŏm!** อย่ามายุ่งกับผม |
| **Get out of here!** | **Àwk pai!** ออกไป |
| **Get lost!** | **Pai hâi pón!** ไปให้พ้น |
| **Go away!** | **Pai glai glai!** ไปไกลไกล |
| **You're noisy!** | **Khun sĭang dang!** คุณเสียงดัง |
| **Be quiet!** | **Phôut bao-bao nòy!** พูดเบา ๆ หน่อย |
| **You're narrow-minded!** | **Khun jai khâaep!** คุณใจแคบ |
| **You're so stingy!** | **Khun khîi-nĭaw mâak!** คุณขี้เหนียวมาก |
| **You're so selfish!** | **Khun hĕn-gàae-tua mâak!** คุณเห็นแก่ตัวมาก |
| **It's better to end things now.** | **Rao lêrrk gan dii gwàa.** เราเลิกกันดีกว่า |

**Let's break up.**          **Lêrrk gan thèr.**
                             เลิกกันเถอะ

**I hope we can still**      **Wǎng wâa rao yang pen**
**be friends.**             **phûean gan dâi.**
                             หวังว่าเรายังเป็นเพื่อน
                             กันได้

Here are some swearwords you can try to use to express your anger and frustration. Beware though that it might have some comical results instead as you're not a native speaker. It's also better to only use this with close Thai friends, unless you're looking for a fight.

**Dumbass  Ngôh/khwaay** โง่/ควาย

**Ngôh** literally means "stupid", while **khwaay** refers to a water buffalo, which can mean a person is being slow and stupid. It is sometimes used to insult your intelligence, but most of the time it just expresses anger.

**What a jerk/Idiot  Pan-yaa-àwn** ปัญญาอ่อน

**Bullshit  Taaw-lǎe** ตอแหล

**Crazy  Bâa/ting-táawng** บ้า/ติงต๊อง

**Bâa** means "crazy", whereas **ting-táawng** is a Thai slang which refers to a goofy, wacky or dorky person.

**Shit!/Damn it!  Mâaeng-éii!** แม่งเอ๊ย

This generally shows that you are angry or annoyed.

**Shut up!  Ngîap pai loey!** เงียบไปเลย

### Fuck/Asshole/Son of a bitch  Hîa  เหี้ย

Hîa refers to a monitor lizard. It is a very common and offensive curse, and also often used to insult a despicable person because this animal symbolizes misfortune.

### Fuck you!  Khuay!  ควย

It literally means "penis" and is considered one of the most vulgar words in Thai. It is typically used amongst Thai males when cursing one another.

### Bastard  (Âi/ii) wen (ไอ้/อี) เวร / (Âi/ii) sàt (ไอ้/อี)  สัตว์

Âi/ii are insulting titles and placed in front of swear words. Âi is used for men, and ii is used for women. These two words are very rude and offensive.

### Whore  Ii-dàawk  อีดอก

### Slutty  Râaet  แรด

Râaet is the Thai word for rhinoceros. This is used on a woman who overtly seeks to attract attention from or aggressively pursues the opposite sex. It is also a term for a woman or girl who has many casual sexual partners, as in English.

# English-Thai Dictionary

## A

about (approximately) **prà-maan** ประมาณ

absolutely, definitely, of course **nâae-naawn** แน่นอน

accident **ù-bàt-tì-hèt** อุบัติเหตุ

accommodation **thîi-phák** ที่พัก

ache **pùat** ปวด

across **trong-khâam** ตรงข้าม

add **sài, phêrm** ใส่, เพิ่ม

address **thîi-yòu** ที่อยู่

adorable (lovable) **nâa-rák** น่ารัก

afraid **glua** กลัว

Africa **Áp-frí-gaa** แอฟริกา

afternoon **taawn-bàay** ตอนบ่าย

again **ìik** อีก

age **aa-yú** อายุ

agree (with someone) **hěn-dûay** เห็นด้วย

air **aa-gàat** อากาศ

airplane **khrûeang-bin** เครื่องบิน

airport **sà-nǎam-bin** สนามบิน

alcohol, liquor (spirits) **lâo** เหล้า

all **tháng-mòt** ทั้งหมด

allergy **pháae** แพ้

almost **gùeap** เกือบ

alone **khon-diaw** คนเดียว

already **láaew** แล้ว

also **dûay** ด้วย

ambulance **rót-phá-yaa-baan** รถพยาบาล

America **À-may-rí-gaa**
อเมริกา

American (person) **Khon-
à-may-rí-gan** คน
อเมริกัน

amusing **tà-lòk** ตลก

and **láe, gàp** และ, กับ

angry **gròht** โกรธ

animal **sàt** สัตว์

annoy **ram-khaan**
รำคาญ

apologize, excuse me
**khǎaw-thôt** ขอโทษ

appearance **nâa-taa**
หน้าตา

April **May-sǎa-yon** เมษายน

arm **khǎen** แขน

arrive **maa-thǔeng** มาถึง

ask (a question) **thǎam**
ถาม

ask for, request **khǎaw** ขอ

assist **châuy** ช่วย

at **thîi** ที่

ATM machine **Tôu-ay-
thii-em** ตู้เอทีเอ็ม

August **Sǐng-hǎa-khom**
สิงหาคม

Australia **Áwt-sà-tray-lia**
ออสเตรเลีย

Australian (person)
**Khon-àwt-sà-tray-lia**
คนออสเตรเลีย

available, free (not busy)
**wâang** ว่าง

## B

back (part of body) **lǎng**
หลัง

banana **glûay** กล้วย

bag (paper or plastic)
**thǔng** ถุง

baht (Thai currency) **bàat**
บาท

bake (to be baked) **òp** อบ

band (of musicians)
**wong-don-trii** วงดนตรี

bank **thá-naa-khaan**
ธนาคาร

Bangkok **Grung-thêp**
กรุงเทพฯ

barber **châang-tàt-phǒm**
ช่างตัดผม

bath **àap-náam** อาบน้ำ

bathroom **hâawng-náam**
ห้องน้ำ

bathtub **àang-àap-náam** อ่างอาบน้ำ

beach, sea **thá-lay** ทะเล

beat (to strike) **tii** ตี

beautiful **sŭay** สวย

because **phráw** เพราะ

bed **tiang** เตียง

bedroom **hâawng-nawn** ห้องนอน

bed sheet **phâa-pou-thîi-nawn** ผ้าปูที่นอน

beef **nûea-wua** เนื้อวัว

before **gàwn** ก่อน

begin, start **rêrm** เริ่ม

behind **khâang-lăng** ข้างหลัง

best **dii-thîi-sùt** ดีที่สุด

better **dii-gwàa** ดีกว่า

between **rá-wàang** ระหว่าง

bicycle **jàk-grà-yaan** จักรยาน

big **yài** ใหญ่

bird **nók** นก

birthday **wan-gèrt** วันเกิด

bit **nít-nòi** นิดหน่อย

black **sĭi-dam** สีดำ

blanket **phâa-hòm** ผ้าห่ม

blood **lûeat** เลือด

blue (dark) **sĭi-náam-ngern** สีน้ำเงิน

blue (light) **sĭi-fáa** สีฟ้า

boat, ship **ruea** เรือ

body **râang-gaay, tua** ร่างกาย, ตัว

boil **tôm** ต้ม

book **năng-sŭue** หนังสือ

bookstore **ráan-năng-sŭe** ร้านหนังสือ

borrow **yuem** ยืม

bottle **khùat** ขวด

bowl **chaam** ชาม

box (a rectangular container) **glàawng** กล่อง

boyfriend, girlfriend **faaen** แฟน

bread **khà-nŏm-pang** ขนมปัง

breakfast **aa-hăan-cháo** อาหารเช้า

bride **jâo-săow** เจ้าสาว

bridegroom **jâo-bàow** เจ้าบ่าว

bridge **sà-phaan** สะพาน

British (person) **Khon-Àng-grìt** คนอังกฤษ

broken **sǐa** เสีย

brother (elder) **phîi-chaay** พี่ชาย

brother (younger) **náawng-chaay** น้องชาย

brown **sǐi-náam-taan** สีน้ำตาล

brush teeth **praaeng-fan** แปรงฟัน

buddy (friend) **phûean** เพื่อน

but **tàe** แต่

butter **noey** เนย

buy **súue** ซื้อ

# C

can **dâi** ได้

Can you…? **…dâi mái?** ได้ไหม

Canada **Khaae-naa-daa** แคนาดา

Canadian (person) **Khon-khaae-naa-daa** คนแคนาดา

candle **thian** เทียน

cannot **mâi-dâi** ไม่ได้

car, automobile **rót** รถ

careful **rá-wang** ระวัง

cash (money) **ngern** เงิน

cat **maaew** แมว

cell phone **muue-thǔue** มือถือ

chair **gôa-îi** เก้าอี้

change (clothes, plans) **plìan** เปลี่ยน

chat **khuy** คุย

cheap (in price) **thòuk** ถูก

cheat **gohng** โกง

chicken **gài** ไก่

child (a son or daughter) **lôuk** ลูก

child (immature person) **dèk** เด็ก

chili pepper **phrík** พริก

China **Jiin** จีน

Chinese (language) **Phaa-sǎa-jiin** ภาษาจีน

Chinese (person) **Khon-jiin** คนจีน

cigarette **bù-rìi** บุหรี่

city **mueang** เมือง

clean **sà-àat** สะอาด

clean **tham-khwaam-sà-àat** ทำความสะอาด

clever **chà-làat** ฉลาด

clothes, clothing **sûea-phâa** เสื้อผ้า

coconut **má-phráow** มะพร้าว

coconut milk **gà-thí** กะทิ

cold (drink) **yen** เย็น

cold (weather) **năow** หนาว

color **sĭi** สี

comb **wĭi** หวี

come **maa** มา

come from **maa-jàak** มาจาก

comfortable **sà-baay** สบาย

computer **cawm-phíew-têr** คอมพิวเตอร์

condition (symptom) **aa-gaan** อาการ

connect **tàw** ต่อ

convenient **sà-dùak** สะดวก

cook **tham-aa-hăan** ทำอาหาร

cool **yen** เย็น

corn **khâow-phôht** ข้าวโพด

cost (price) **raa-khaa** ราคา

cousin **lôuk-phîi-lôuk-náawng** ลูกพี่ลูกน้อง

country **prà-thêt** ประเทศ

cow **wua** วัว

crab **pou** ปู

crash **chon** ชน

crazy, mad **bâa** บ้า

create, build, to **sâang** สร้าง

credit card **bàt-khray-dìt** บัตรเครดิต

cry **ráawng-hâi** ร้องไห้

cucumber **taaeng-gwaa** แตงกวา

cup **thûay** ถ้วย

cushion (pillow) **măawn** หมอน

cut **tàt** ตัด

cut (injure) **phlăe** แผล

cute **nâa-rák** น่ารัก

# D

dance **tên** เต้น

danger, dangerous **an-tà-raay** อันตราย

daughter **lôuk-săow** ลูกสาว

day **wan** วัน

day off **wan-yùt** วันหยุด

dead **taay** ตาย

December **Than-waa-khom** ธันวาคม

delay **cháa** ช้า

delicious **à-ròy** อร่อย

deliver **sòng** ส่ง

dentist **than-tà-phâaet** (formal), **măaw-fan** (common) ทันตแพทย์, หมอฟัน

depart **àwk** ออก

department store **hâang** ห้าง

desk **tóh** โต๊ะ

dessert, sweet **khà-nŏm**, **khăawng-wăan** ขนม, ของหวาน

detergent (washing powder) **phŏng-sák-fâwk** ผงซักฟอก

die (become dead) **taay** ตาย

die (stop operating) **sĭa** เสีย

difficult **yâak** ยาก

dinner **aa-hăan-yen** อาหารเย็น

dirty **sòk-gà-pròk** สกปรก

discount **lót** ลด

disease **rôhk** โรค

dish, plate **jaan** จาน

dislike **mâi-châawp** ไม่ชอบ

dive **dam-náam** ดำน้ำ

do **tham** ทำ

Don't! (do something) **Yàa!** อย่า

doctor **măaw** หมอ

dog **măa** หมา

dollar **daawn-lâa** ดอลลาร์

door **prà-tou** ประตู

down **long** ลง

downstairs **khâang-lâang** ข้างล่าง

drink **dùuem** ดื่ม

drive **khàp** ขับ

driver **khon-khàp-rót** คนขับรถ

drunk (affected by alcohol) **mao** เมา

dry **hâeng** แห้ง

duck **pèt** เป็ด

## E

ears **hǒu** หู

easy **ngâay** ง่าย

eat **gin** กิน

eggs **khài** ไข่

eight **pàaet** แปด

elephant **cháang** ช้าง

eleven **sìp-èt** สิบเอ็ด

email **ii-meo** อีเมล์

embassy **sà-thǎan-thôut** สถานทูต

embrace, hug **gàawt** กอด

empty **wâang** ว่าง

engaged (to be married) **mân** หมั้น

English (language) **Phaa-sǎa-ang-grìt** ภาษา อังกฤษ

enjoy, fun **sà-nùk** สนุก

enough, sufficient **phaaw** พอ

enter, to **khâo** เข้า

entrance **thaang-khâo** ทางเข้า

errand **thú-rá** ธุระ

evening **taawn-yen** ตอนเย็น

every day **thúk-wan** ทุกวัน

everyone **thúk-khon** ทุกคน

everything **thúk-yàang** ทุกอย่าง

exchange (money) **lâek-ngern** แลกเงิน

excited **tùuen-tên** ตื่น เต้น

exercise, to **àwk-gam-lang gaay** ออกกำลังกาย

expensive **phaaeng** แพง

express, urgent **dùan** ด่วน

extra **phí-sèt** พิเศษ

extremely **thîi-sùt** ที่สุด

eye **taa** ตา

# F

face **nǎa** หน้า

faint **pen-lom** เป็นลม

fake (an imitation)
  **plaawm** ปลอม

fall **tòk** ตก

fall over **lóm** ล้ม

family **khrâawp-khrua**
  ครอบครัว

fan **phát-lom** พัดลม

fancy **rǒu** หรู

far **glai** ไกล

farmer **chaow-naa** ชาวนา

fast **rew** เร็ว

fat **ûan** อ้วน

father **phâaw** พ่อ

fear **glua** กลัว

fee **khâa** ค่า

fever **pen-khâi** เป็นไข้

fiancé, fiancée **khôu-mân**
  คู่หมั้น

finger **níw** นิ้ว

fire **fai** ไฟ

fish **plaa** ปลา

fish sauce **náam-plaa**
  น้ำปลา

five **hâa** ห้า

fix, repair **sâawm** ซ่อม

flashlight, torch **fai-chǎay**
  ไฟฉาย

flight (an airline) **thîaw-
  bin** เที่ยวบิน

flirt **jìip** จีบ

flour **pâaeng** แป้ง

flower **dàawk-mái**
  ดอกไม้

flu, influenza **khâi-wàt-yài**
  ไข้หวัดใหญ่

fly (insect) **má-laaeng-
  wan** แมลงวัน

fly **bin** บิน

fond of **châawp** ชอบ

food **aa-hǎan** อาหาร

foot **tháo** เท้า

foreign, overseas **tàang-
  prà-thêt** ต่างประเทศ

forest **pàa** ป่า

forget **luuem** ลืม

fork **sâawm** ส้อม

four **sìi** สี่

France **Fà-ràng-sèt**
  ฝรั่งเศส

French (language) **Phaa-săa-fà-ràng-sèt** ภาษาฝรั่งเศส

French (person) **Khon-fà-ràng-sèt** คนฝรั่งเศส

Friday **Wan-sùk** วันศุกร์

friend **phûean** เพื่อน

frightened **tòk-jai** ตกใจ

from **jàak** จาก

front **nâa** หน้า

fruit **phŏn-lá-mái** ผลไม้

fry **thâawt** ทอด

full **ìm** อิ่ม

fun **sà-nùk** สนุก

funny **tà-lòk** ตลก

# G

garbage, rubbish, trash **khà-yà** ขยะ

garden, yard **sŭan** สวน

garlic **grà-thiam** กระเทียม

gas, gasoline, petrol **náam-man** น้ำมัน

gas station **pám-náam-man** ปั๊มน้ำมัน

generous **jai-dii** ใจดี

German (language) **Phaa-săa-yer-rá-man** ภาษาเยอรมัน

German (person) **Khon-săa-yer-rá-man** คนเยอรมัน

Germany **Yer-rá-man** เยอรมัน

get (receive) **dâi** ได้

get off (e.g., a bus) **long** ลง

get on (e.g., a bus) **khûen** ขึ้น

get up **tùuen-naawn** ตื่นนอน

get well **hăay** หาย

gift, present **khăawng-khwăn** ของขวัญ

girl **dèk-phôu-yĭng** เด็กผู้หญิง

girlfriend, boyfriend **faaen** แฟน

give **hâi** ให้

glad **dii-jai** ดีใจ

glass **gâaew** แก้ว

glasses **wâaen-taa** แว่นตา

glue **gaow** กาว

go **pai** ไป

go back **glàp** กลับ

go home **glàp-bâan** กลับบ้าน

go out **pai-thîaw** ไปเที่ยว

go straight ahead **trong-pai** ตรงไป

good **dii** ดี

grandchild **lăan** หลาน

granddaughter **lăan-săow** หลานสาว

grandfather (maternal) **taa** ตา

grandfather (paternal) **pòu** ปู่

grandmother (maternal) **yaay** ยาย

grandmother (paternal) **yâa** ย่า

grandson **lăan-chaay** หลานชาย

grape **à-ngùn** องุ่น

grass **yâa** หญ้า

grateful **khàawp-khun** ขอบคุณ

gray **sĭi-thao** สีเทา

green **sĭi-khĭaw** สีเขียว

green bean **thùa-fàk-yaow** ถั่วฝักยาว

grill **yàang** ย่าง

guava **fà-ràng** ฝรั่ง

## H

hair **phŏm** ผม

hair cut **tàt-phŏm** ตัดผม

half **khrûeng** ครึ่ง

hand **muue** มือ

handsome **làaw** หล่อ

happy **dii-jai** ดีใจ

hard (to be difficult) **yâak** ยาก

hard (solid) **khăeng** แข็ง

hardworking, diligent **khà-yăn** ขยัน

hat, cap **mùak** หมวก

have, has **mii** มี

he **khăo** เขา

head **hŭa** หัว

hear **dâi-yin** ได้ยิน

heart attack **hŭa-jai-waay** หัวใจวาย

heavy **nàk** หนัก

Hello **Sà-wàt-dii** สวัสดี

Hello (on phone) **Han-lŏh** ฮัลโหล

help **chûay** ช่วย

her **khăo** เขา

hers **khăawng-khăo** ของเขา

here **thîi-nîi** ที่นี่

him **khăo** เขา

his **khăawng-khăo** ของเขา

hit **tii** ตี

home **bâan** บ้าน

honey **náam-phûeng** น้ำผึ้ง

horrible (frightening) **nâa-glua** น่ากลัว

hospital **rohng-phá-yaa-baan** โรงพยาบาล

hot **ráawn** ร้อน

hotel **rohng-raem** โรงแรม

hour **chûa-mohng** ชั่วโมง

house **bâan** บ้าน

housekeeper, housemaid **mâe-bâan** แม่บ้าน

how **yang-ngai** ยังไง

how many **gìi** กี่

how much **thâo-rài** เท่าไร

how old **kìi-pii** กี่ปี

huge **yài** ใหญ่

humid **chúuen** ชื้น

humorous, funny **tà-lòk** ตลก

hundred **róy** ร้อย

hungry **hǐw** หิว

Hurry up! **Rew-rew!** เร็ว ๆ

husband **săa-mii** สามี

hurt (injured), sore **jèp** เจ็บ

# I

I [FEMALE] **Chăn** ฉัน

I [MALE] **Phŏm** ผม

ice **náam-khăeng** น้ำแข็ง

ice cream **ai-sà-khriim** ไอศกรีม

iced water **náam-yen** น้ำเย็น

ill, sick **mâi-sà-baay** ไม่สบาย

image **rôup-phâap** รูปภาพ

impatient **jai-ráawn**
ใจร้อน

important **săm-khan**
สำคัญ

impossible **pen-pai-mâi-dâi** เป็นไปไม่ได้

impressive **prà-tháp-jai**
ประทับใจ

in **nai** ใน

in front **khâang-nâa**
ข้างหน้า

inconvenient **mâi-sà-dùak** ไม่สะดวก

India **In-dia** อินเดีย

Indian (person) **Khon-in-dia** คนอินเดีย

inexpensive **mâi-phaaeng**
ไม่แพง

injection **chìit-yaa** ฉีดยา

injured **bàat-jèp** บาดเจ็บ

insects **má-laaeng** แมลง

inside **khâang-nai** ข้างใน

interested, to be **sŏn-jai**
ไม่สนใจ

Internet **In-ter-nèt**
อินเตอร์เน็ต

interpret, translate **plaae**
แปล

intersection **sìi-yâaek**
สีแยก

invite (informal) **chuan**
ชวน

invite (formal) **cherrn** เชิญ

island **gàw** เกาะ

Italy **Ì-taa-lîi** อิตาลี

Italian (language) **Phaa-săa-ì-taa-lîi** ภาษาอิตาลี

Italian (person) **Khon-ì-taa-lîi** คนอิตาลี

itchy **khan** คัน

## J

jam **yaaem** แยม

January **Mók-gà-raa-khom** มกราคม

Japan **Yîi-pùn** ญี่ปุ่น

Japanese (language)
**Phaa-săa-yîi-pùn**
ภาษาญี่ปุ่น

Japanese (person) **Khon-yîi-pùn** คนญี่ปุ่น

jeans **gaang-geng-yiin**
กางเกงยีน

joke (with someone)
**phôut-lên** พูดเล่น

juice **náam-phǒn-lá-mái**
น้ำผลไม้

July **Gà-rá-gà-daa-khom**
กรกฎาคม

jump **grà-dòht** กระโดด

June **Mí-thù-naa-yon**
มิถุนายน

jungle **pàa** ป่า

## K

kale **khá-náa** คะน้า

keep **gèp** เก็บ

kettle **gaa-náam** กาน้ำ

key (for a room) **gun-jaae**
กุญแจ

kick **tè** เตะ

kid (child) **dèk** เด็ก

kilogram **gì-loh-gram**
กิโลกรัม

kind (personality) **jai-dii**
ใจดี

kiss, to **jòup** จูบ

kitchen **khrua** ครัว

Korea **Gao-lǐi** เกาหลี

Korean (language) **Phaa-sǎa-gao-lǐi** ภาษาเกาหลี

Korean (person) **Khon-gao-lǐi** คนเกาหลี

knee **khào** เข่า

knife **mîit** มีด

know (to possess knowledge) **rúu** รู้

know (familiar with someone) **rúu-jàk** รู้จัก

## L

lamp **khohm-fai** โคมไฟ

language **phaa-sǎa** ภาษา

last **thîi láew** ที่แล้ว

large, big **yài** ใหญ่

late **sǎay** สาย

late at night **dùek** ดึก

laugh **hǔa-ráw** หัวเราะ

laundry **sák-phâa** ซักผ้า

learn, study **rian** เรียน

leather **nǎng** หนัง

leave a message **fàak-khâaw-khwaam** ฝากข้อความ

left (direction) **sáay** ซ้าย

leg **khǎa** ขา

lemongrass **tà-khrái**
ตะไคร้

letter (mail) **jòt-mǎay**
จดหมาย

lettuce **phàk-gàat-khǎow** ผักกาดขาว

lie **goh-hòk** โกหก

lie down **nawn** นอน

life **chii-wít** ชีวิต

lift, raise **yók** ยก

light (bright) **sà-wàang** สว่าง

light (lamp) **fai** ไฟ

like **châawp** ชอบ

lime **má-naow** มะนาว

lip **rim-fǐi-pàak** ริม ฝีปาก

liquor, alcohol **lâo** เหล้า

listen **fang** ฟัง

little **nít-nòy, nóy** นิด หน่อย, น้อย

live **yòu** อยู่

long (length) **yaow** ยาว

look at **dou** ดู

look for, search, look up **hǎa** หา

lost (something, some-one) **hǎay** หาย

lost (direction) **lǒng-thaang** หลงทาง

lot (a large amount) **mâak, yér** มาก, เยอะ

loud **dang** ดัง

love **rák** รัก

lovely, adorable **nâa-rák** น่ารัก

lucky **chôhk-dii** โชคดี

luggage, bag, suitcase **grà-pǎo** กระเป๋า

lunch **aa-hǎan-thîang** อาหารเที่ยง

# M

make **tham** ทำ

makeup (cosmetics) **khrûeang-sǎm-aang** เครื่องสำอาง

man, men **phôu-chaay** ผู้ชาย

manager **phôu-jàt-gaan** ผู้จัดการ

mango **má-mûang** มะม่วง

mangosteen (fruit) **mang-khút** มังคุด

manicure **châang-tham-lép** ช่างทำเล็บ

many **mâak** มาก

map **phǎaen-thîi** แผนที่

March **Mii-naa-khom** มีนาคม

market **tà-làat** ตลาด

marry, get married **tàaeng-ngaan** แต่งงาน

massage **nûat** นวด

mattress **thîi-nawn** ที่นอน

May **Phrúet-sà-phaa-khom** พฤษภาคม

me [FEMALE] **chǎn** ฉัน

me [MALE] **phǒm** ผม

medicine, drug **yaa** ยา

meet **phóp** พบ

meeting (a conference) **prà-chum** ประชุม

message **khâaw-khwaam** ข้อความ

midday **thîang-wan** เที่ยงวัน

midnight **thîang-khuen** เที่ยงคืน

milk (also used for a woman's breasts) **nom** นม

million **láan** ล้าน

mind **jai** ใจ

mine [FEMALE] **khǎawng-chǎn** ของฉัน

mine [MALE] **khǎawng-phǒm** ของผม

minibus (with two bench seats) **rót-sǎawng-thǎaew** รถสองแถว

minute **naa-thii** นาที

mirror, a **grà-jòk** กระจก

miss (someone) **khít-thǔeng** คิดถึง

mist, fog **mǎawk** หมอก

mix, blend, to **phà-sǒm** ผสม

mobile phone **muue-thǔue** มือถือ

Monday **Wan-jan** วันจันทร์

money **ngern** เงิน

monk (a Buddhist monk) **phrá** พระ

monkey **ling** ลิง

month **duean** เดือน

more than (comparative form of adjectives) **mâak-gwàa** มากกว่า

morning **taawn-cháo** ตอนเช้า

mother, mom **mâae** แม่

mountain **phou-khǎo** ภูเขา

moustache **nùat** หนวด

mouth **pàak** ปาก

movie **nǎng** หนัง

Mr., Mrs., Ms., **Khun** คุณ

MSG (monosodium glutamate) **phǒng-chou-rót** ผงชูรส

museum **phí-phít-thá-phan** พิพิธภัณฑ์

mushroom(s) **hèt** เห็ด

music **phleng, don-trii** เพลง, ดนตรี

## N

nail (finger, toe) **lép** เล็บ

name **chûue** ชื่อ

nation, country **prà-thêt** ประเทศ

navy blue **sǐi-náam-ngern** สีน้ำเงิน

near **glâi** ใกล้

neck **khaaw** คอ

neighbor **phûean-bâan** เพื่อนบ้าน

never mind **mâi-pen-rai** ไม่เป็นไร

new, to be **mài** ใหม่

news **khàow** ข่าว

newspaper **nǎng-sǔue-phim** หนังสือพิมพ์

New Zealand **Niw-sii-laaen** นิวซีแลนด์

nice, good **dii** ดี

nickname **chûue-lên** ชื่อเล่น

night time **taawn-khâm** ตอนค่ำ

nine **gâo** เก้า

nineteen **sìp-gâo** สิบเก้า

ninety **gâo-sìp** เก้าสิบ

no, not **mâi, mâi-châi** ไม่, ไม่ใช่

noise, a sound **sǐang** เสียง

noisy, loud noise **sǐang-dang** เสียงดัง

noodles **gǔay-tîaw** ก๋วยเตี๋ยว

noon **thîang-wan** เที่ยงวัน

normal **pòk-gà-tì** ปกติ

nose **jà-mòuk** จมูก

not at all **mâi-loey**
ไม่เลย

notebook **sà-mùt** สมุด

November **Phrúet-sà-jì-gaa-yon** พฤศจิกายน

now **taawn-níi** ตอนนี้

number **berr** เบอร์

nurse **phá-yaa-baan**
พยาบาล

# O

o'clock **mohng** โมง

October **Tù-laa-khom**
ตุลาคม

of, belong to **khǎawng**
ของ

often **bòy** บ่อย

oil **náam-man** น้ำมัน

old (long use) **gào** เก่า

on **bon** บน

one **nùeng** หนึ่ง

one hundred **nùeng-róy**
หนึ่งร้อย

one thousand **nùeng-phan** หนึ่งพัน

one hundred thousand
**nùeng-sǎaen** หนึ่งแสน

one-way (ticket) **thîaw-diaw** เที่ยวเดียว

onion **hǔa-hǎawm** หัว
หอม

open, turn on **pèrt** เปิด

opposite **trong-khâam**
ตรงข้าม

or **rǔe** หรือ

orange **sôm** ส้ม

order **sàng** สั่ง

other **ùuen** อื่น

our **khǎawng-rao** ของ
เรา

outside **khâang-nâawk**
ข้างนอก

oven **tao-òp** เตาอบ

ox **wua** วัว

# P

pain, painful **jèp** เจ็บ

pajamas **chút-naawn** ชุด
นอน

pan, frying pan **grà-thá**
กระทะ

pants, trousers **gaang-geng** กางเกง

papaya **má-lá-gaaw** มะละกอ

papaya salad **sôm-tam** ส้มตำ

paper **grà-dàat** กระดาษ

parents **phâaw-mâae** พ่อแม่

park (garden) **sǔan** สวน

passport **nǎng-sǔue-derrn-thaang** หนังสือเดินทาง

patient (personality) **jai-yen** ใจเย็น

pay **jàay** จ่าย

peanut **thùa** ถั่ว

pen **pàak-gaa** ปากกา

pencil **din-sǎaw** ดินสอ

people, person **khon** คน

pepper (chili pepper) **phrík** พริก

perfume **náam-hǎwm** น้ำหอม

pet (animal) **sàt-líang** สัตว์เลี้ยง

petrol, gasoline **náam-man** น้ำมัน

picture, photo **rôup, phâap** รูป, ภาพ

pig, pork **mǒu** หมู

pill(s) **yaa** ยา

pillow, cushion **mǎawn** หมอน

pineapple **sàp-pà-rót** สับปะรด

pink **sǐi-chom-phou** สีชมพู

plan **phǎaen** แผน

plane **khrûeang-bin** เครื่องบิน

plate, dish **jaan** จาน

play (verb) **lên** เล่น

playful **khîi-lên** ขี้เล่น

please **chûay** ช่วย

pleased **dii-jai** ดีใจ

police **tam-rùat** ตำรวจ

police station **sà-thǎa-nii-tam-rùat** สถานีตำรวจ

port, harbor **thâa-ruea** ท่าเรือ

post office **prai-sà-nii** ไปรษณีย์

prawn, shrimp **gûng** กุ้ง

present (gift) **khǎawng-khwǎn** ของขวัญ

pretty **sǔay** สวย

price **raa-khaa** ราคา

problem **pan-hǎa** ปัญหา

professor **aa-jaan** อาจารย์

promise **sǎn-yaa** สัญญา

province **jang-wàt** จังหวัด

pull (verb) **dueng** ดึง

punctual, on time **trong-way-laa** ตรงเวลา

purple **sǐi-mûang** สีม่วง

purse **grá-pǎo** กระเป๋า

put on, wear **sài** ใส่

## Q

question **kham-thǎam** คำถาม

quickly **rew** เร็ว

quiet **ngîap** เงียบ

quit, give up **lêrk** เลิก

quit, resign **laa-àwk** ลาออก

## R

rabbit **grà-tàay** กระต่าย

radio **wít-thá-yú** วิทยุ

rain (noun) **fǒn** ฝน

rain (verb) **fǒn-tòk** ฝนตก

raise, breed **lîang** เลี้ยง

rash **phùuen** ผื่น

rat, mouse **nǒu** หนู

read **àan** อ่าน

really (adverb) **jing-jing, mâak** จริง ๆ, มาก

ready **phrâwm** พร้อม

receive **ráp** รับ

red **sǐi-daaeng** สีแดง

reduce **lót** ลด

refrigerator **tôu-yen** ตู้เย็น

regret (to feel sorry) **sǐa-jai** เสียใจ

rent **châo** เช่า

reply, answer **tàawp** ตอบ

request **khǎaw** ขอ

reserve (a room) **jawng** จอง

rest, relax **phák-phàwn** พักผ่อน

restaurant **ráan-aa-hǎan** ร้านอาหาร

restroom (bathroom) **hâwng-náam** ห้องน้ำ

return, go back **glàp** กลับ

return a call **thoh-glàp** โทรกลับ

rice (food) **khâow** ข้าว

ride (bicycle, animal) **khìi** ขี่

right (side) **khwǎa** ขวา

ring (jewelry) **wǎen** แหวน

rinse, wash **láang** ล้าง

river **mâae-náam** แม่น้ำ

road **thà-nǒn** ถนน

roast, grill **yâang** ย่าง

room (house, hotel) **hâawng** ห้อง

rose apple **chom-pôu** ชมพู่

round trip (ticket) **pai-glàp** ไปกลับ

run **wîng** วิ่ง

## S

sad **sǐa-jai** เสียใจ

sale (reduced prices) **lót-raa-khaa** ลดราคา

salt **gluea** เกลือ

salty (taste) **khem** เค็ม

same, the **mǔean** เหมือน

sandals **raawng-tháo-tàe** รองเท้าแตะ

Saturday **Wan-sǎo** วันเสาร์

say, speak **phôut** พูด

school **rohng-rian** โรงเรียน

sea **thá-lay** ทะเล

seafood **aa-hǎan-thá-lay** อาหารทะเล

search for **hǎa** หา

season **rúe-dou** ฤดู

seasoning, ingredient **khrûeang-prung** เครื่องปรุง

seat **thîi-nâng** ที่นั่ง

see **hěn** เห็น

sell **khǎay** ขาย

send **sòng** ส่ง

send an email **sòng-ii-meo** ส่งอีเมล์

September **Gan-yaa-yon** กันยายน

seven **jèt** เจ็ด

several, many **lǎay** หลาย

shampoo **yaa-sà-phǒm** ยาสระผม

shave **gohn** โกน

she **khǎo** เขา

shelf, shelves **chán** ชั้น

shoes **raawng-tháo** รองเท้า

shop, store **ráan** ร้าน

short (length) **sân** สั้น

short (height) **tîa** เตี้ย

shower (or bath) **àap-náam** อาบน้ำ

shrimp, prawn **gûng** กุ้ง

shut, to close **pìt** ปิด

shy **aay** (feeling), **khîi-aay** (personality) อาย, ขี้อาย

siblings **phîi-náawng** พี่น้อง

sick, ill **mâi-sà-baay** ไม่สบาย

sing **ráawng-phleng** ร้องเพลง

single (not married) **sòht** โสด

sink (in the bathroom) **àang-láang-nâa** อ่างล้างหน้า

sink (for washing dishes) **àang-láang-jaan** อ่างล้างจาน

sister (older) **phîi-sǎow** พี่สาว

sister (younger) **náawng-sǎow** น้องสาว

sit **nâng** นั่ง

six **hòk** หก

skillful **gèng** เก่ง

skinny **phǎawm** ผอม

skirt **grà-prohng** กระโปรง

sleep **naawn** นอน

sleepy **ngûang-naawn** ง่วงนอน

slow, slowly **cháa** ช้า

small (size) **lék** เล็ก

smart **chà-làat** ฉลาด

smile **yím** ยิ้ม

snack **khà-nǒm** ขนม

snake **ngou** งู

snow **hì-má** หิมะ

soap **sà-bòu** สบู่

socks **thǔng-tháo** ถุงเท้า

sofa **soh-faa** โซฟา

soldier **thá-hăan** ทหาร

son **lôuk-chaay** ลูกชาย

song **phleng** เพลง

sore, painful **jèp** เจ็บ

sorry (apology) **khăaw-thôt** ขอโทษ

sorry (regret) **sĭa-jai** เสียใจ

sour (taste) **prîaw** เปรี้ยว

spicy **phèt** เผ็ด

spoon **cháawn** ช้อน

stairs, steps **ban-dai** บันได

stand **yuen** ยืน

state **rát** รัฐ

steam **nûeng** นึ่ง

sticky rice **khâow-nĭaw** ข้าวเหนียว

stink **mĕn** เหม็น

stir-fry **phàt** ผัด

stop, halt **yùt** หยุด

stop (pause for a short time while traveling) **jàawt** จอด

stove **tao** เตา

straight ahead **trong-pai** ตรงไป

street, road **thà-nŏn** ถนน

strong **khăeng-raaeng** แข็งแรง

student (school) **nák-rian** นักเรียน

student (university) **nák-sùek-săa** นักศึกษา

study, learn **rian** เรียน

sugar **náam-taan** น้ำตาล

Sunday **Wan-aa-thít** วันอาทิตย์

sure **nâae-jai** แน่ใจ

surname, last name **naam-sà-gun** นามสกุล

sweet **wăan** หวาน

swim **wâay-náam** ว่ายน้ำ

# T

table **tóh** โต๊ะ

take off **thàawt** ถอด

talk **phôut, khuy** พูด, คุย

tall **sŏung** สูง

taste (verb) **chim** ชิม

tasty **à-ròy** อร่อย

tea **chaa, náam-chaa** ชา, น้ำชา

teach **sǎawn** สอน

teacher **khrou** ครู

teeth, tooth **fan** ฟัน

telephone (n) **thoh-rá-sàp** โทรศัพท์

television **thii-wii** ทีวี

tell (someone) **bàawk** บอก

temple (Buddhist) **wát** วัด

ten **sìp** สิบ

ten thousand **mùen** หมื่น

Thai (language) **Phaa-sǎa-thai** ภาษาไทย

Thai (person) **Khon-thai** คนไทย

Thailand **Prà-thêt-thai** ประเทศไทย

thank, thank you **khàawp-khun** ขอบคุณ

there (at that place) **thîi-nân** ที่นั่น

there is, there are **mii** มี

they **khǎo** เขา

thin (appearance) **phǎawm** ผอม

think **khít** คิด

think of **khít-thǔeng** คิดถึง

thirsty **hǐw-náam** หิวน้ำ

thousand **phan** พัน

three **sǎam** สาม

Thursday **Wan-phá-rúe-hàt** วันพฤหัส

ticket **tǔa** ตั๋ว

time **way-laa** เวลา

tired, exhausted **nùeay** เหนื่อย

today **wan-níi** วันนี้

tofu, soyabean **tâo-hôu** เต้าหู้

toilet **sûam** ส้วม

tomato **má-khǔea-thêt** มะเขือเทศ

tomorrow **phrûng-níi** พรุ่งนี้

too, also **dûay** ด้วย

toothbrush **praaeng-sǐi-fan** แปรงสีฟัน

toothpaste **yaa-sǐi-fan** ยาสีฟัน

torch, flashlight **fai-chǎay** ไฟฉาย

towel **phâa-chét-tua** ผ้าเช็ดตัว

town **mueang** เมือง

traffic jam **rót-tìt** รถติด

traffic light **fai-daaeng** ไฟแดง

train **rót-fai** รถไฟ

train station **sà-thǎa-nii-rót-fai** สถานีรถไฟ

tree **tôn-mái** ต้นไม้

true **jing** จริง

try on (clothes) **laawng** ลอง

Tuesday **Wan-ang-khaan** วันอังคาร

turn left **líaw-sáay** เลี้ยวซ้าย

turn right **líaw-khwǎa** เลี้ยวขวา

twelve **sìp-sǎawng** สิบสอง

twenty **yîi- sìp** ยี่สิบ

two **sǎawng** สอง

## U

ugly **nâa-glìat** น่าเกลียด

umbrella **rôm** ร่ม

uncomfortable **mâi-sà-baay** ไม่สบาย

under, underneath **tâi** ใต้

understand **khâo-jai** เข้าใจ

unfortunate **chôhk-ráay** โชคร้าย

university **má-hǎa-wít-thá-yaa-lai** มหาวิทยาลัย

up **khûen** ขึ้น

upstairs **khâang-bon** ข้างบน

urgent **dùan** ด่วน

use **chái** ใช้

used to **khoey** เคย

usually **pà-gà-tì, pòk-gà-tì** ปกติ

## V

vacant **wâang** ว่าง

vacation, holiday **wan-yùt** วันหยุด

van (vehicle) **rót-tôu** รถตู้

vegetable **phàk** ผัก

vegetarian **mang-sà-wí-rát** มังสวิรัติ

vegetarian (Chinese) **jay** เจ

very **mâak** มาก

vomit (formal) **aa-jian**
อาเจียน

vomit (informal) **ûak**
อ้วก

## W

wait for **raaw** รอ

wait a moment **raaw-dǐaw** รอเดี๋ยว

wake up **tùuen-naawn**
ตื่นนอน

walk **derrn** เดิน

want to (do something)
**tâawng-gaan** (formal),
**yàak** (informal)
ต้องการ, อยาก

want (to get something)
**yàak-dâi** อยากได้

warm (weather) **ùn** อุ่น

wash **láang** ล้าง

wash face **láang-nâa** ล้าง
หน้า

wash hair **sà-phǒm**
สระผม

wash dishes **láang-jaan**
ล้างจาน

wash clothes **sák-phâa**
ซักผ้า

wash hands **láang-muue**
ล้างมือ

watch (a show, a movie)
**dou** ดู

water **náam** น้ำ

waterfall **náam-tòk**
น้ำตก

we, us **rao** เรา

wear **sài** ใส่

weather **aa-kàat** อากาศ

wedding **ngaan-tàaeng-ngaan** งานแต่งงาน

Wednesday **Wan-pút**
วันพุธ

week **aa-thít** อาทิตย์

weight **náam-nák** น้ำหนัก

well, good **dii, sà-baay-dii** ดี, สบายดี

well (skillful) **gèng** เก่ง

well-cooked, well-done
**sùk** สุก

wet **pìak** เปียก

what **à-rai** อะไร

what time **kìi-mohng**
กี่โมง

when **mûea-rài** เมื่อไร

where **thîi-nǎi** ที่ไหน

which one (an object)
**an-năi** อันไหน

which one (an animal)
**tua-năi** ตัวไหน

white **sĭi-khăow** สีขาว

who **khrai** ใคร

why **tham-mai** ทำไม

wife **phan-rá-yaa** ภรรยา

wind **lom** ลม

window **nâa-tàang**
หน้าต่าง

winter **rúe-dou-năow**
ฤดูหนาว

woman, female **phôu-
yĭng** ผู้หญิง

work, job **ngaan** งาน

work (verb) **tham-ngaan**
ทำงาน

would like, may I have?
**khăaw** ขอ

write **khĭan** เขียน

wrong (incorrect) **phìt** ผิด

**Y**

year **pii** ปี

yellow **sĭi-lŭeang** สี
เหลือง

yes **châi** ใช่

yesterday **mûea-waan-níi**
เมื่อวานนี้

you **khun** คุณ

younger brother
**náawng-chaay** น้องชาย

younger sister **náawng-
săao** น้องสาว

your **khăawng-khun**
ของคุณ

**Z**

zebra **máa-laay** ม้าลาย

zero **sŏun** ศูนย์

zoo **sŭan-sàt** สวนสัตว์

## ABOUT TUTTLE
### "Books to Span the East and West"

Our core mission at Tuttle Publishing is to create books which bring people together one page at a time. Tuttle was founded in 1832 in the small New England town of Rutland, Vermont (USA). Our fundamental values remain as strong today as they were then—to publish best-in-class books informing the English-speaking world about the countries and peoples of Asia. The world has become a smaller place today and Asia's economic, cultural and political influence has expanded, yet the need for meaningful dialogue and information about this diverse region has never been greater. Since 1948, Tuttle has been a leader in publishing books on the cultures, arts, cuisines, languages and literatures of Asia. Our authors and photographers have won numerous awards and Tuttle has published thousands of books on subjects ranging from martial arts to paper crafts. We welcome you to explore the wealth of information available on Asia at **www.tuttlepublishing.com**.

Published by Tuttle Publishing, an imprint of Periplus Editions (HK) Ltd.

www.tuttlepublishing.com

Copyright © 1988 Charles E. Tuttle Publishing Co. Inc.
Copyright © 2003, 2015, 2017 Periplus Editions (HK) Ltd.
Illustrations by Suman S Roy

ISBN 978-0-8048-4821-3
LCC No: 2017942022

20 19 18 17   5 4 3 2 1   1707RR
Printed in China

TUTTLE PUBLISHING® is a registered trademark of Tuttle Publishing, a division of Periplus Editions (HK) Ltd.

**Distributed by:**

**North America, Latin America & Europe**
Tuttle Publishing
364 Innovation Drive
North Clarendon, VT 05759-9436, USA
Tel: 1 (802) 773 8930
Fax: 1 (802) 773 6993
info@tuttlepublishing.com
www.tuttlepublishing.com

**Japan**
Tuttle Publishing
Yaekari Building 3F 5-4-12 Osaki
Shinagawa-ku Tokyo 141-0032 Japan
Tel: (81) 3 5437 0171
Fax: (81) 3 5437 0755
sales@tuttle.co.jp
www.tuttle.co.jp

**Asia Pacific**
Berkeley Books Pte. Ltd.
61 Tai Seng Avenue #02-12
Singapore 534167
Tel: (65) 6280-1330
Fax: (65) 6280-6290
inquiries@periplus.com.sg
www.periplus.com